Breakfast in London

—

Dinner in Paris

© Kristina BABI, 2024

Editor: Emma Mansfield
Photographer: Jekaterina Prihodko
Designer: Olga Mikheenkova

Self published

ISBN 978-1-3999-9763-8

KRISTINABABI**.COM**

LOVE STORY
WITH RECIPES

Breakfast in London

—

Dinner in Paris

KRISTINA
BABI

Contents

TRUE FRENCH AND BRITISH CUISINE
15 Lyonnais Bouchons
16 Potato Gratin
19 French Home Cooking
21 Custard & Gravy: Two Must-Have Ingredients in British Cuisine

VIBRANT MARKETS
26 French Food Markets
30 Borough Market

MY FAVOURITE LIQUEUR, WINE, CHAMPAGNE AND PUNCH
36 Crème de Cassis
39 Beaujolais Nouveaux
42 Vintage Champagne
45 PIMM's in the Sun and Beyond

UNFORGETTABLE PLACES
48 Hearty Salads in Grasse
52 Sardine Festivals in Martigues

DELIGHTFUL DESSERTS
57 Calissons d'Aix
58 Nougat
61 Spiced Honey Cake
63 Alice, Meet the Pudding

EDIBLE FLOWERS
68 Violet
72 Lavender
75 Elderflower Cordial

PROVENCAL ADVENTURES
79 Truffles
82 Cavaillon Melons

PERHAPS THE ULTIMATE DELICACY
88 Pan-Seared Foie Gras
90 Foie Gras Terrine

LEGENDARY SOUPS
95 Bouillabaisse
98 Onion Soup
101 Smoked Haddock Soup from Scotland

THE CROWN JEWEL
106 Bûche de Noël
109 Operation: Saving the Bûches de Noël
113 Duck for Christmas

SAY "CHEESE"
118 Perfect Savoyard Fondue
121 My Find: Morbier Cheese
125 Roquefort or Shropshire Blue for Breakfast?
127 Stinking Bishop: Expectations vs Reality

FASCINATING FRENCH GEOGRAPHY
132 Five Reasons to Visit the French Riviera in Winter
136 France Forever

SCOTTISH HOLIDAYS
142 Scotland
144 Haggis, or Through Scotland on the Handbrake
145 My Love, Nighttime Edinburgh

WHO SAID "CHOCOLATE"?
149 Chocolate Mood
152 Brownies
156 Chocolate Mousse and Life's Turmoil

ROASTING FANATIC
161 Tian – Recipe for My Favourite Provençal Roasted Vegetables
163 Sunday Roast
164 Concept: One-Tin Roasting

OPPOSITES ATTRACT
171 Orange Marmalade
174 My Impressions of London and Marmite

SEAFOOD SENSATIONS
178 Langoustines from the Bay Outside
181 New Year's Lobster
182 Aioli

FIVE O'CLOCK TEA
187 Afternoon Tea at F&M
190 Earl Grey: the Story of Our Relationship

THE PERFECT DINNER
194 Onion Confit
198 Irish Stew

FRENCH CLUB CHALLENGES
203 Galettes des Rois
206 Mini Quiches for the French Club

ENGLAND CALLING
210 Strawberry Fields of the Beatles
214 British Culinary Names of French Origin
218 Picnic on the Beach: Always with Fish and Chips
220 Top Five London Restaurants
222 Untouristy England in the Cotswolds
226 Burgers: Yes, Please!
230 Strangest British Dishes
232 British Pub Culture and Shepherd's Pie

Recipes

Potato Gratin	17
Leek Gratin	20
Custard	22
Gravy	23
Marinated Artichokes	29
Quinoa, Mango and Sugar Snap Pea Salad	32-33
Duck in a Reduced Orange Sauce	38
Hot Oysters	40
Provencal-Style Sea Bream with Tapenade	44
Mango and Prawn Salad with Sweet Chili Sauce	51
Frozen Nougat	59
Spiced Honey Cake	62
Sticky Toffee Pudding	64-65
Violet Cake	71
Lavender Crème Brûlée	73
Summer Punch with Elderflower Cordial	74
Truffle Mash	81
Pan-Seared Giant Prawns with Melon	85

Pan-Seared Foie Gras	89	Orange Marmalade with Whisky	172
Foie Gras Terrine	91	Aioli	183
Easy Bouillabaisse	96-97	Classic English Scones	189
Onion Soup	100	Liver with Onion and Date Confit	196-197
Scottish Soup Cullen Skink	103	Irish Stew	199
Bûche de Noël	110-111	Galettes des Rois	205
Roasted Duck with Orange Glaze	114	Mini Quiches	207
Fondue	119	Strawberry Cupcakes	212-213
Tartiflette	122	Yorkshire Pudding	217
Mango Lime Marmalade	124	Garden Risotto	225
Baked Camembert	128-129	Grilled Pineapple Burger	228
Lemon Curd	134-135	Shepherd's Pie	233
Onion Confit	139		
Chocolate Cake	150		
Brownies	154-155		
Chocolate Mousse	156		
Tian	161-162		
English Sausages Baked with Fennel, Red Onion and Apples	166-167		

Introduction

France. I fell head over heels for this country like a giddy young girl. Newly married to an MBA student at the INSEAD business school, brimming with colourful expectations, I eagerly embraced the beauty, flavours and aromas with wide-eyed wonder and a heart full of joy. And, oh! The beauty seemed endless. In that first year, we travelled far and wide – picturesque villages, towns, cities, castles, valleys and hills. We tasted, savoured, absorbed and marvelled. The romance of it all swept us off our feet, with flowers and trees blooming in a kaleidoscope of colours, making that year feel like an extended honeymoon.

Then reality hit and we reluctantly returned to the dreary weekdays, dreading the thought of leaving. So, whenever we could break free from the chaos of life, we found ourselves back in France – initially just the two of us, then with our daughter, and later with our son. We even brought our extended family along on holidays. It felt like there was no place on Earth quite like it. Our love for France was so deep-rooted that we contemplated making it our home.

However, my husband approached the potential move with caution and spent months delving into the intricacies of the French tax code. Gradually, I realised our yearning for France was waning. Then the pandemic struck and, before we knew it, we found ourselves on the last flight to London just before air travel ground to a halt.

England. It was a place I had never quite pictured myself in. Landing here so unexpectedly, I went through stages of surprise, denial and finally acceptance. Initially, I compared the romantic lavender fields of Provence to the quintessential English pubs, which were worlds apart. But I soon discovered the unique delights of English lavender and so much more.

Nevertheless, the longing for France still lingered deep in my heart, and I sought traces of its presence everywhere. In one particular London district, the French influence is unmistakable: luxury boutiques, restaurants and a legendary cheese shop. I found myself drawn here whenever possible and those visits made me glow with joy.

"Dis-moi ce que tu manges, je te dirai ce que tu es"
Brillat-Savarin

Perhaps I initially hoped to find my beloved France in the UK, but I've come to cherish the delicate balance I've struck in embracing both countries. Whether I'm comparing French and British cuisine or singing the praises of British dishes in one of my viral videos, emotions always run high.

I mistakenly held onto certain biases, but reality has proved me wrong. From delicious Irish stew to Scottish haggis and the wonderful range of British puddings… Even fish and chips can be a culinary delight with some refined seasoning.

I have a passion for cooking and have gathered a treasure trove of gastronomic experiences from both countries, and I wholeheartedly share the best of both in this book. I've adopted *l'art de vivre* from the French – a philosophy that extends to their food. From the British, I've embraced their creativity and knack for incorporating the best of other cultures and cuisines, resulting in a delightful fusion and modern recipes that I enjoy adapting in my kitchen in this vibrant cosmopolitan city I now call home.

This book is designed to captivate your imagination. Picture yourself on the Eurostar, travelling from London to Paris and back again with every turn of the page. Each story comes with a recipe just waiting to be savoured. You may well find yourself hitting pause and rushing to the supermarket or kitchen to create a culinary masterpiece.

Every dish I recommend has been tried, tested and approved by my most discerning critic, my partner in all adventures and fellow Francophile – my beloved husband. Though reluctantly, he was my first and steadfast listener and editor, and for this I am eternally grateful.

If you doubt his objectivity, think again. Before writing this book, I sought the support of like-minded individuals and received glowing reviews on my blog. I've hosted numerous guests, French and British among them, even some unique Franco-British enthusiasts from our local French circle.

Also my French teacher, a role model and source of inspiration since our early days in the Fontainebleau forest, has had a profound impact on me. In our lessons, we

> "Tell me what you eat, I will tell you who you are"
> Brillat-Savarin

tirelessly discuss French dishes – ingredients, pairings, presentation – and delve into the rich culinary traditions of France.

But most importantly, my mother played a pivotal role in shaping my palate. Her creativity and culinary enthusiasm held such significance for me that I feel compelled to pass this legacy on to my own daughter.

Family support has enveloped me like a warm blanket, carrying me through each phase of this journey. Thanks to their active involvement, the vision crystallised and unfolded like a kaleidoscope of memories and emotions.

If you're wondering why I'm sharing my culinary discoveries from the UK and France, it's simple: to spread the joy and light I've experienced. Writing has soothed my soul, just like watching a documentary about a three-Michelin-star restaurant in Paris near the Rodin Museum, a place I yearn to visit.

I've been fortunate to channel my passion for French gastronomy and my openness to new experiences in the UK, aiming to inspire you with a smile and a zest for culinary creativity.

Enjoy and *bon appétit!*

TRUE FRENCH AND BRITISH CUISINE

Lyonnais Bouchons
\bouchons de Lyon\

Explore the charming streets of Lyon and you'll discover the hidden gems known as *"bouchons"* – cosy eateries with small tables draped in classic red-chequered tablecloths. These authentic establishments are nestled in the pedestrian centre, featuring low ceilings adorned with ancient wooden beams.

Lyon is renowned for offering a true taste of French cuisine, with locals considering it the epitome of culinary authenticity, surpassing even Paris. It's a compelling reason to plan a visit to Lyon and experience the local gastronomic delights firsthand.

During our initial visit, seeking shelter from the rain, we stumbled upon a *bouchon* and secured the last table for two. At that time, it was just the two of us – something which is now hard to believe! We opened the menu and there it was – the most wonderful onion soup (*soupe à l'oignon*) you can dream of, as well as the perfect side dish – potato gratin (*gratin dauphinois*). For the main course, I chose tender pink veal kidneys (*rognons de veau*) with succulent green beans – simple, but unforgettable. My husband bravely went for the *andouillette*. If you are unfamiliar with this robust dish but are adventurous and open to new experiences, make your decision wisely: it's a coarse-grained sausage made from pork intestines. It has a charm of its own, but it's not for the fainthearted.

The friendly atmosphere and lively banter in Lyon's bouchons add to the overall charm of the dining experience. You can engage in conversation with the welcoming staff and neighbouring diners, creating a convivial ambiance that will leave you in high spirits for the rest of the evening. Each visit to Lyon's *bouchons* is a joyful memory that beckons you back for more delectable moments.

Potato Gratin
\gratin dauphinois\

As I slowly open my eyes in a homely Victorian house in North London, I find myself in a dream-like state. Memories of Lyon and its enchanting restaurants linger in my mind – a fleeting vision I wish to hold on to. I recall being asked about the secret to the perfect gratin, a question that had eluded me amidst the busyness of life until these serene "homey" weekends unfolded.

We didn't go outside due to the weather, with the rain and wind creating a symphony of sounds. Darkness enveloped both day and night, while the wind danced playfully on the fragile English windows. Seeking warmth and comfort, we lit an improvised fire – a video playing on the TV screen in front of the dormant hearth.

Amidst the crackling of logs and purring of the cat on the sofa, the children immersed in their gadgets and my husband lost in his computer, I found solace in the kitchen. Recalling the gratin recipe taught to me by my favourite French teacher during our early days in France, I embarked on preparing a meal, pairing honey and soy sauce-glazed chicken with gratin dauphinois. The familiar aroma filled the kitchen, evoking memories of culinary adventures past!

The children are often reluctant to leave their screens and gather at the table. However, once they took the first bite, they eagerly devoured the entire plate. I wish there were more of these gloomy homey days!

POTATO GRATIN

Here are the key steps:

Instructions

1. Use a mandoline for thin, uniform potato slices. Avoid washing the potatoes after slicing to retain the starch for binding.

2. Crush the garlic and use it to grease the baking dish along with some butter.

3. Layer the potatoes, season with salt and pepper, and sprinkle grated nutmeg between each layer.

4. Cover the potatoes with a mixture of whole milk and low-fat cream in a 2:1 ratio. Bake for 2.5 hours at 150°C, ensuring the bottom doesn't burn. Check the potatoes are cooked through using a knife.

French Home Cooking
\cuisine familiale française\

You might be surprised, but French cuisine is not just about the famous chef Alain Ducasse.

Yes, we often think of France as refined and sophisticated in taste and aromas. Yes, the French are all about delicate and beautiful food, peacefully enjoying long meals from an early age, and learning so many interesting and useful things about food. But in this amazing country, there are both famous chefs and cooking enthusiasts – *cuisiniers et cuisinières* – all creating culinary magic.

The amateurs inspire me just as much as the pros. They are always so interested in how I cook, like it's the million-dollar question. They appreciate every little detail, invention, tip and trick. I draw the utmost pleasure from discussing dinner with the French.

For me, the top five dishes of French home cooking are:

- *le hachis parmentier*, a tasty potato and meat pie
- *les endives au jambon*, ham-wrapped endives
- *la tarte aux pommes et boudin noir*, a unique apple and black pudding pie
- *le gratin de poireaux*, a mouthwatering leek gratin
- *la blanquette de veau*, tender veal with veggies in a creamy sauce

Whip up a delicious leek gratin with this easy and vibrant recipe!

LEEK GRATIN

Ingredients

1 kg leeks
250 ml milk
100 ml double cream
20 g flour
40 g butter
100 g grated Gruyère cheese
Salt and pepper
Nutmeg

Instructions

1. Bring a large pot of salted water to the boil. Trim the leeks, then slice and rinse them. Tie them with string and boil for 10 minutes. Preheat the oven to 240°C.

2. Make a creamy bechamel sauce: melt the butter, whisk in the flour and add the cold milk, salt, pepper and nutmeg to taste. Simmer for 10 minutes.

3. Grease a baking dish, layer in the dried leeks, pour over the sauce and sprinkle with cheese. Bake for 10 minutes, then dig in!

Custard and Gravy:
TWO MUST-HAVE INGREDIENTS IN BRITISH CUISINE

Of course, this is just my personal impression, not a statement of fact. But the effect it has had on me was so bright and mesmerising that I can't help but share it. British chefs have two magical sauces in their arsenal – one salty and one sweet, but both brimming with flavour.

Almost no dessert, and especially no pudding, is complete without a thick vanilla custard. The French call it *crème anglaise*, or English cream, elevating it to universal status.

From my first encounter with England, I had a strong feeling that this sauce was truly versatile. You can pour it over a hot cherry pie to make its taste less sour and more intense, layer it on top of fruit jelly, or use it as a filling in tarts or even cupcakes. The possibilities are endless.

Likewise, no Sunday roast or plate of bangers and mash is complete without a meaty gravy. This sauce ramps up the flavour by 200%. Essentially, it's a rich meaty sauce, but with a touch of sophistication, especially when infused with a splash of red wine.

CUSTARD

Custard is easy to make at home.

Ingredients

- 2 eggs
- 3 tbsp cornflour
- 3 cups milk
- 3 tbsp sugar (adjust to taste)
- 1 tsp vanilla extract

Instructions

1. Whisk the eggs, cornflour and milk in a saucepan.

2. Place over a low heat and continue whisking until thickened and smooth.

3. Add the sugar and vanilla extract.

GRAVY

Ingredients

- 1 glass (200 ml) red wine
- 3 tbsp cornflour
- 600 ml chicken stock
- 2 tbsp redcurrant jelly

Instructions

1. Start by mixing the cornflour with 3 tbsp of red wine until smooth, then add the rest of the wine.

2. Heat the chicken stock and add the wine mixture and redcurrant jelly. Keep stirring until the liquid thickens.

3. Store in the fridge for up to 2 days, covered with cling film. Reheat until bubbles form before serving.

4. For an extra boost of flavour, add up to 200 ml of pan juices from the roasted meat, chicken or turkey that you will be serving with the gravy.

VIBRANT MARKETS

French Food Markets
\marchés hebdomadaires\

The topic is so exciting, and the memories are so vivid, that I don't even know where to start. In short, the weekly food markets in France (often on weekends, but sometimes midweek, in each town on its chosen day) are a wonderful experience.

The abundance of produce itself is a great source of creative inspiration: how should I cook this in order to fully savour it? Which cheese to choose? Which is the most aromatic and flavourful *saucisson*? Oh, what a beautiful artichoke, what should I do with it?

And the fish markets in seaside towns? They are like music, springtime, a balm for the heart! Each stall bustling with excitement and queues. The sellers skilfully fillet and clean the fish for you, showing it off and exchanging jokes with the customers as they work.

I remember once deciding to buy a couple of slices of beef liver from the butcher. "Thick or not so thick?" he asked, enquiring how I wanted the slices, and it seemed that no matter my answer a nod and gesture indicating something in the middle was enough. A one-man show then began as he expertly manoeuvred the knife, cutting out the tiniest veins. I had never encountered such delicate handling of liver before. And let the whole world wait!

By the way, it's best to visit the market with a strong companion: dealing with the consequences of a hearty appetite alone will be more than you can manage when it comes to carrying your purchases to the car.

MARINATED ARTICHOKES

If you happen to find artichokes at the market, especially small and tender ones, here's how to prepare them.

Instructions

1. Remove the tough outer leaves, starting from the centre and working your way down. Trim the stem, leaving about 3-4 cm, and remove any tough fibres with a knife or vegetable peeler. Cut off almost half of the bud, ensuring no thick outer leaves remain.

2. Repeat with 4 more artichokes. Place the prepared buds in water with lemon slices to prevent oxidation. Boil in salted water for about 10 minutes until tender. Test by piercing the base with a knife.

3. Dry the artichokes, then scoop out the fluffy centres with a spoon.

4. Make the marinade by mixing olive oil, balsamic vinegar, crushed garlic and chopped parsley. The marinade should complement the artichokes' flavour.

5. Chill for at least 5 hours. Serve in a salad with rocket and cherry tomatoes, on warm bruschetta with goat's cheese, or simply enjoy them on their own!

Borough Market

I was in a whirlwind of excitement and anticipation, unsure of what to expect, but eager to visit this legendary London food market. It is said that all the renowned chefs shop there, which certainly creates a grand impression.

Located directly under a railway bridge, the market resonates with the constant clatter of wheels – creating an incredibly atmospheric setting. But what stands out most are the extraordinary gastronomic delights on offer, almost like museum exhibits.

Let me start by sharing the joy of finally finding and purchasing my beloved French cheese, Saint-Félicien! It was a moment of pure delight after giving up on finding it.

The market offers an enchanting selection of spices that you can smoothly and slowly peruse, your eyes being drawn to each name. Discovering lavender and violet syrup in charming little bottles makes you feel like an alchemist rather than a cook.

You might try and learn about rose-pistachio or coconut-cardamom with cashew as well as peanut butter. Your head spins, and you end up getting both.

And where there are cheeses, there are also sausages – even donkey sausage! Oh my!

The queue for fresh Colombian coffee is long and the choice of smoothie ingredients, including blends of pineapple, mango, banana, wheatgrass, barley grass, flaxseed, apple and orange juice, is mesmerising. What a delicious treat!

On Sunday afternoons, the market bustles with crowds enjoying hot street food like paella and mushroom risotto. It is a hub for foodies and tasting enthusiasts, as well as hedonists.

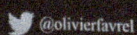

I brought my husband along for company and we had a fantastic time, escaping from the daily grind.

As a result, I found myself returning to Borough Market repeatedly, finding any excuse to indulge in the delightful aromas, colours and textures of the wonderful products. Here's a recipe inspired by the amazing offerings from this market.

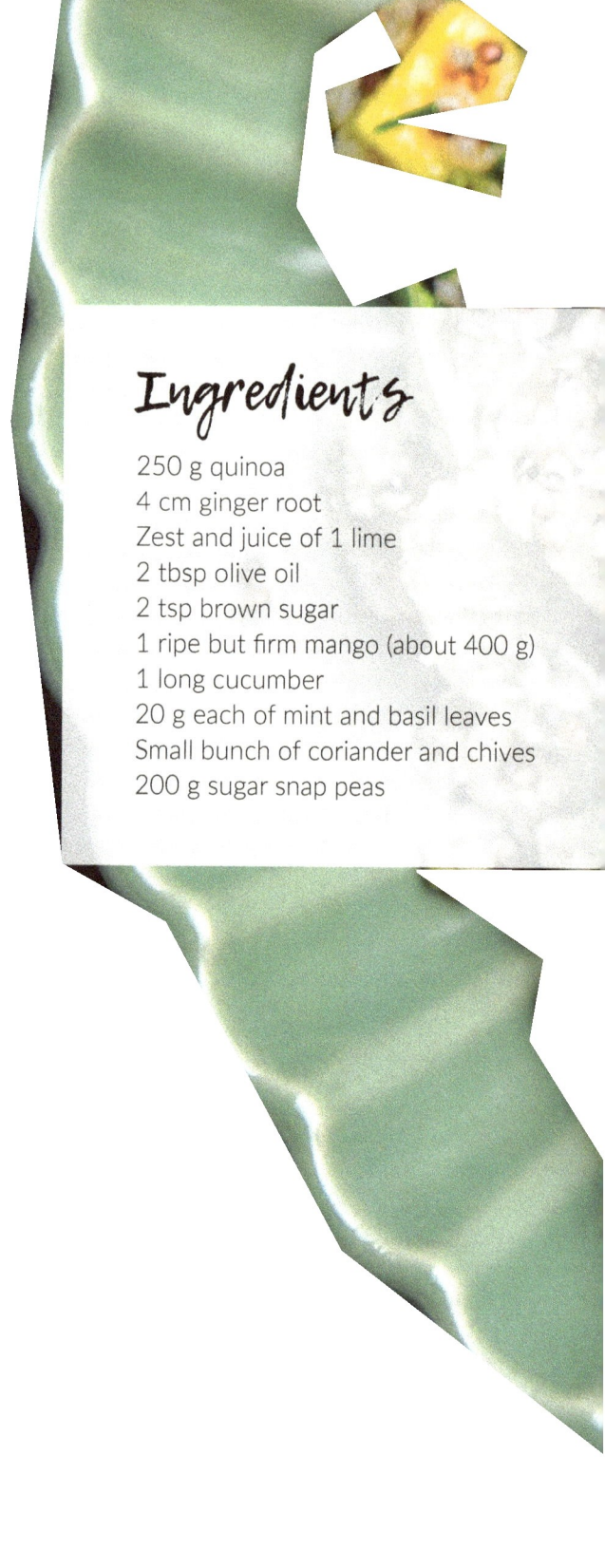

Ingredients

250 g quinoa
4 cm ginger root
Zest and juice of 1 lime
2 tbsp olive oil
2 tsp brown sugar
1 ripe but firm mango (about 400 g)
1 long cucumber
20 g each of mint and basil leaves
Small bunch of coriander and chives
200 g sugar snap peas

QUINOA, MANGO AND SUGAR SNAP PEA SALAD

Instructions

1. Prepare the quinoa by rinsing it and cooking it in a saucepan with water in a 1:4 ratio. Bring to the boil and add salt, then reduce the heat and simmer for 20 minutes until sprouted. Drain and cool.

2. In a large bowl, make the dressing by grating ginger and adding lime zest, juice, olive oil, sugar, salt and pepper.

3. Peel and dice the mango, then add it to the dressing bowl.

4. Peel the cucumber, remove the watery seeds, dice and add to the bowl.

5. Chop the herbs, slice the sugar snap peas and mix into the salad.

6. Finally, add the cooled quinoa, mix well and adjust the seasoning to taste.

7. The salad can be prepared in advance, up to 3-4 hours before serving.

MY FAVOURITE LIQUEUR, WINE, CHAMPAGNE AND PUNCH

Crème de Cassis

Burgundy: Vézelay, Beaune, Nuits-Saint-Georges, Dijon… Travelling the iconic wine route, we stumbled upon *crème de cassis*, a vibrant and luscious liqueur made from blackcurrants.

Planted in the 19th century after the phylloxera invasion, blackcurrants are now a defining element of modern Burgundy, alongside wine, snails and mustard.

Isn't it marvellous that the mayor of Dijon once mixed *crème de cassis* with aligote white wine, creating a delectable cocktail known as Kir? While Kir Royal, made with Champagne, is more renowned, I prefer the original version with white wine for that authentic touch.

This delightful combination has inspired other variations, like using peach or grapefruit liqueur. The latter, when added to rosé wine, is a speciality in Grasse, a charming town near Cannes on the French Riviera.

I also enjoy using blackcurrant liqueur in cooking, such as for a simple duck sauce. After my trip to Burgundy, I fell in love with *magret de canard* and *crème de cassis*, and decided to blend them to create a delicious dish.

The result? A glorious dish that has graced our menu for years. I turn to this recipe when I'm craving enjoyment and praise.

Simple yet sensational, "my duck" never fails to impress with its touch of French elegance. And my husband always raves, "It's like dining at a Michelin-starred restaurant!"

DUCK IN A REDUCED ORANGE SAUCE

Ingredients

4 duck breast fillets with skin
200 ml orange juice
50 ml blackcurrant liqueur
Salt and pepper

Instructions

I season the duck with salt and pepper, then sear it in its own fat skin-side down until golden. Next, I pour in the orange juice and add the blackcurrant liqueur. I simmer the sauce until thickened, gently cooking the duck in the sauce on both sides.

Beaujolais Nouveaux

Every year, wine enthusiasts celebrate a major event – the arrival of the new Beaujolais harvest. This eagerly awaited occasion is joyfully celebrated around the world, but especially in France. Now, the burning question is: what should accompany a bottle of this young wine?

Traditionally, it's a platter of cured meats (*charcuterie*) and cheeses. For this special occasion, the popular pork sausage known as *une rosette lyonnaise* is a must, along with young and incredibly aromatic cheeses. According to a friend of mine who is an expert in wine and food pairing, the best cheeses to enjoy with Beaujolais are:

Brillat-savarin — a delicate cow's milk cheese with white mould, offering a creamy taste with hints of bitterness and mushrooms.

Saint-marcellin — a small, round and incredibly aromatic cheese with fruity, mushroomy and nutty flavours.

Beaufort d'été — a dense, almost hole-free hard cheese with a subtle nutty taste, sometimes called the "prince of Gruyères".

Cervelle de canut — a Lyon-originated soft cheese dip with garlic and herbs.

Raclette — a dense semi-hard pressed cheese with an intense aroma and rich flavour.

You can also pair Beaujolais with lightly cooked meats or bruschetta with sun-dried tomatoes.

And for a delightful surprise: try Beaujolais Nouveau with oysters to break the stereotype that they only go with white wine. You can even prepare them hot for a unique twist on this classic pairing.

HOT OYSTERS

Ingredients

12 oysters
75 g butter at room temperature
8–10 sprigs of parsley
8–10 sprigs of coriander
1 small shallot
A pinch of salt and freshly ground pepper
A bag of coarse salt

Instructions

Open the oysters, drain the excess liquid and place them on a bed of salt in an oven-proof dish. Finely chop the parsley, coriander and shallot, then season with salt and pepper. In a bowl, mix the herbs, shallot and butter with a fork. Top each oyster with a bit of the mixture and bake in the oven for 3–4 minutes. Serve immediately.

Vintage Champagne
\champagne millésimé\

As the festive season approaches, I select the champagne for New Year's Eve. Let me share my perspective and maybe help you make your decision.

My initial thoughts: sticking with the classics – renowned houses like Veuve Clicquot, Dom Pérignon and Louis Roederer. While undeniably excellent, they are also traditional. Year after year, the cellar masters of these big names blend old and new vintages to maintain a consistent taste. Meanwhile, smaller champagne houses craft their own unique blends, making each year's champagne distinct.

Here, I am quoting our wine-expert friend from a tasting, where we learnt to appreciate the difference. Not just between mass-produced and artisanal champagne, but also between aged and young vintages. He leans towards champagnes that are around 20 years old. Some may prefer the boldness of young wines, sparkling included, while others find them a bit rough around the edges.

Each champagne is unique, even down to the size of the bubbles. Surprisingly, in one case, we discovered a bold aroma of blue cheese mould and a hint of the countryside – uncivilised yet refined, showcasing the vintage's individuality.

At a tasting a few years back, we fell in love with Ayala Brut Millésimé 1996 from Côte des Blancs – a region known for producing lively champagnes with delicate aromas, which are both refined and elegant.

This time, I'm tempted to try Ayala Brut Millésimé 1999. It's said to pair well with scallop carpaccio or dishes featuring white fish such as turbot, sea bass or sea bream. A delightful addition to a festive menu! And if you're looking for a delicious but different option, a whole sea bream never fails to impress.

PROVENCAL-STYLE SEA BREAM WITH TAPENADE

Ingredients

2 medium-sized sea bream
4 medium tomatoes
3 sprigs of basil
Salt and freshly ground pepper
100 g pitted black olives
1 tablespoon capers
2 cloves of garlic
20 g (2–3 pieces) anchovies (optional)
Olive oil

Instructions

1. Slice the tomatoes, then season with salt and pepper. Clean and gut the fish, then rinse it inside and out.

2. Make the tapenade by blending the olives, capers and garlic. Add anchovies cautiously if desired. Drizzle in 2–3 tablespoons of olive oil and mix well.

3. Season the fish with salt and pepper, brush with olive oil and place in a baking dish. Spread the tapenade on top like a cosy blanket. Arrange the tomatoes on top.

4. Bake at 200°C for 15 minutes. Garnish with basil leaves before serving.

PIMM's in the Sun
AND BEYOND

Looking out at the blossoming Regent's Park, I'm amazed: in just two weeks, it has transformed into a floral paradise. Even the freshly mowed meadows near the water are adorned with delicate daisies, seemingly planted by nature itself. The natural beauty and allure, surrounded by lush trees and vibrant flower beds, make it feel like the gardener went all out, creating a magical display. Spring is in full bloom and the scents are enchanting.

In the heart of the park lies my favourite café where I can choose a sunny table with a QR code for easy ordering. And there it is on the drinks menu – the classic PIMM's cocktail. Instantly, memories flood back from the summer when I volunteered at the lively fair in my local area of Highgate. The PIMM's stand consistently drew the longest queues.

PIMM's is like an English take on a light punch, with a touch of soapiness, blended with tonic water or lemonade and a mix of fruits – strawberries taking the spotlight.

My fondness for PIMM's grew as I watched it flow freely at that fair, bringing with it joy and smiles. It's like a taste of sunshine, even if you find yourself reminiscing about summer on a chilly winter evening in the local pub, taking a brief break and leaving the kids to themselves at home. It's a fleeting sense of freedom and a little indulgence.

As summer rolls around, it's time to embrace cocktail season and garden gatherings. While we may lack a garden at our home, there are still ways to enjoy the season – strolling in parks, having picnics or visiting friends!

UNFORGETTABLE PLACES

\salades gourmandes à Grasse\

Hearty Salads
IN GRASSE

I can't wait to rave about my absolute favourite city – Grasse. Just 10 kilometres from Cannes, up in the mountains, it offers spectacular sea views, winding streets, warm-coloured houses, an abundance of cats, perfume museums, cosy restaurants, a fountain in the square, and a range of gourmet and souvenir shops.

Our first visit there as students left us enamoured for life. Back then, the first iPhone was just about to come out and I managed to fill up my digital camera's memory in a day. When I accidentally formatted the memory card while looking through the photos that evening, I cried my heart out, fearing I might never see that beauty again.

To complete the experience, we returned to Grasse the next day. We strolled around until we stumbled upon a sunny cafe serving les salades gourmandes – a glorious concept where your plate is loaded with melon and jambon cru, tabbouleh, veggies, capers, lettuce and bruschetta with baked goat's cheese. This generous hearty salad was a meal in itself, and I later noticed that many French people opted for the "salad plus drink" set menu during working lunches.

One lunchtime, a lovely French acquaintance, Evelyne, introduced me to the idea of a hearty salad and nothing more. The combinations of ingredients are endless, limited only by your imagination. Here are a few intriguing options:

Salade périgourdine — a classic from southwestern France with caramelised chicken gizzards, fried bacon, potatoes, frisée lettuce, green beans, pine nuts, walnut oil, wine vinegar and mustard.

Salade méditerranéenne — a Mediterranean delight with couscous, olive oil, cherry tomatoes, white wine vinegar, lentils, feta cheese, pitted Kalamata olives, basil, salt and pepper.

Assiette italienne — an Italian treat featuring rocket, speck, marinated peppers, sun-dried tomatoes, Parmesan slices, pine nuts, olive oil and balsamic glaze.

Salade de boeuf à la mangue — a refreshing mix of thinly sliced roast beef, mango, toasted cashews, coriander, basil, lime juice, olive oil, salt, pepper and a pinch of chilli flakes.

However, my most frequent and popular homemade salad in London is this one...

MANGO AND PRAWN SALAD WITH SWEET CHILLI SAUCE

Ingredients

1 pack (120 g) rocket
1 pack (400 g) cherry tomatoes
2 ripe avocados
1 large mango or 2 small ones (about 450 g)
1 small pack (200 g) raw frozen prawns
Salt, pepper, olive oil
Sweet chilli sauce
Parmesan cheese (70 g)

Instructions

1. Start by laying a bed of rocket on a plate and topping it with cherry tomatoes and sliced avocados. Season with salt and a drizzle of olive oil. Place the mango slices on top.

2. Heat some olive oil in a pan and cook the prawns until pink on all sides. Season with salt and pepper. Pour in the sweet chilli sauce, enough to coat the prawns, and simmer until it thickens.

3. Plate the prawns, drizzle with the sauce and sprinkle shaved Parmesan over the salad.

\sardinades\
Sardine Festivals
IN MARTIGUES

Once, by a stroke of luck, we found ourselves in Martigues – a city northwest of Marseille on the shores of a vast saltwater lake – where we stumbled upon a bustling and crowded festival. Tables and chairs were set up on what had been a car park, with every seat taken and long queues forming at the stalls. It turned out to be an annual celebration dedicated to sardines, and all the local fish lovers were joyfully partaking in the festivities. "How delightful", we thought, and wholeheartedly joined in the celebrations.

One reason for the festival's popularity may have been the 10 euro menu: a plate of grilled sardines, a plastic cup of white wine and a slice of bread. Alternatively, in another version (*moulinade*, not *sardinade*), which we experienced a couple of years later in Brusc, *moules marinières* were cooked right on the waterfront in large cauldrons over open flames, served with chips and that same plastic cup of wine.

We also noticed a charming detail: both the groups at the tables and the queue of people waiting for the next batch of sardines were engaged in light-hearted chit-chat. After a few glasses of wine, everyone was in high spirits and no one minded if someone joined the queue or conversation.

The tables were so packed that many guests found themselves sitting on the edge of the waterfront next to the boats. We too embraced this scenario, feeling a unique sense of camaraderie and joy. Unfortunately, someone nearby ended up taking an unplanned dip in the water!

A small and unassuming fish, dancing well into the night and an abundance of food – that's the essence of a lively French festival.

DELIGHTFUL DESSERTS

Calissons d'Aix

Have you ever tried the delightful calissons from Aix-en-Provence? First, you experience a light crunch through the royal icing, which reveals a soft paste resembling marzipan but made from fresh candied melon, zesty orange peel and tender blanched almonds. The base is a delicate layer of potato starch and water, which is, of course, edible.

These mini pastries are shaped like almonds or, as some say, a woman's eye. This comparison isn't arbitrary. Legend has it that this sweet treat was created by a royal confectioner in 1454 during a feast celebrating the marriage of Good King René and Jeanne de Laval, who was 35 years younger than her groom. After tasting them, she smiled for the first time and asked, "What is this?" The king was moved and exclaimed, *"Di calin soun!"* (in Provençal) or in French, *"Ce sont des câlins!"* which means "These are kisses!"

Every time the owner visited us at the house we rented on the coast southeast of Aix, she brought a box of calissons, a sweet gesture which led to a wonderful friendship. It was impossible to resist her calissons! She was a warm host and clearly cherished them as the perfect treat, even though those small boxes of sweets weren't cheap. The price reflects the quality ingredients and the time-consuming preparation.

I highly recommend visiting a pastry boutique or a factory near Aix to taste this sweet speciality, where each piece embodies Provencal *art de vivre*. My top tip: choose sturdy packaging, as calissons are delicate and the icing can get crushed during transport.

Nougat

Our introduction to French nougat began with a visit to the luxurious sweet shops in Burgundian Beaune. The vibrant displays left us in awe, making it hard to decide between dark or light nougat with their array of colours and fillings.

However, the true roots of this delicacy lie in Montélimar, nestled in northern Provence, shortly after Orange on the road from Avignon to Lyon. Here, in one of the oldest artisanal establishments "Arnaud Soubeyran", you'll find the Nougat Museum, where the history of this sweet treat made from honey and almonds dates back to the 17th century.

In the charming town of Sault, a lesser-known gem in Provence, nougat is crafted from delicately aromatic lavender honey. We embarked on a scenic drive from Aix, winding our way to the base of Mont Ventoux to admire the stunning violet-blue landscapes of the lavender fields. Our journey was rewarded with the discovery of the delectable Nougat André Boyer, an authentic nougat boutique.

A handy tip: opt for soft nougat – *nougat tendre* – for a more satisfying chewing experience.

We also fell head over heels for *nougat glacé*, or frozen nougat. After tasting it once, we found ourselves unsuccessfully searching for this delectable dessert in other restaurants. Here's my simple recipe to recreate this frozen delight.

FROZEN NOUGAT

Ingredients

3 eggs
300 ml whipping cream
120 g sugar
100 g liquid honey
150 g almonds
75 g pistachios

Instructions

Roast the pistachios and almonds in a pan, sprinkle with sugar and let them caramelise. Separate the egg whites from the yolks. Warm the honey. Beat the egg whites until frothy, then pour in the warm honey, stirring well. Combine the remaining sugar with the yolks, beat and mix with the egg whites. Whip the cream and fold it into the egg and honey mixture. Finally, add the coarsely chopped nuts. Pour the mixture into a loaf pan lined with cling film for easy removal and freeze for at least 12 hours.

Spiced Honey Cake
\pain d'épices\

There is a time of year when winter has not yet arrived, but we've already dug up a Christmas tree from the forest, positioned it by the window and decorated it. As darkness falls, we light up the garlands, and there's the tree, sprinkled with snow and bringing joy as the festive season approaches.

I gaze at it and reminisce about Christmas Eve in Bourron-Marlotte, a magical little town near Fontainebleau, where we spent a year at business school. One late evening, we ventured out into the crisp cold air, strolling through the winding cobblestone streets and finding ourselves completely alone. Our neighbours were all snug at home, with most of them lighting their fireplaces. The air was filled with the comforting scent of smoke and the festive lights added to the enchanting atmosphere. As the school year drew to a close, I soaked up that moment with all my heart – we had never felt so content as we did in that first year in France.

Now let me share with you a Christmas baking tradition that is closely linked to the festive season but can be enjoyed all year round: the delightful *pain d'épices*, a fragrant honey cake with a rich spiced flavour that you really must try baking yourself.

SPICED HONEY CAKE

Ingredients

To begin, you'll need to prepare a special mix of spices, which includes:
20 g ground cinnamon
2 star anise
10 cloves
10 g coriander seeds
7 g aniseed
1 dessert spoon ground ginger
¼ teaspoon ground nutmeg

Next, gather the ingredients for the cake:
160 g flour
160 g blossom honey
60 g butter
1-2 dessert spoons of the prepared spice mix
7 g baking soda
70 g milk
65 g cane sugar

Instructions

Preheat your oven to 155°C. Melt the butter and leave it to cool. Gently melt the honey over a low heat. Mix the flour, spices and baking soda. Combine the honey with the milk, then add the butter and the dry mix. Stir well and then incorporate the cane sugar. Grease and lightly flour a standard-sized loaf tin, then pour in the mixture. Bake for 1 hour without opening the oven door to prevent the cake from sinking or cracking. Check the cake is cooked using a wooden skewer, then allow it to cool in the tin on a wire rack. The cake can be stored for several days wrapped in baking paper.

Alice, Meet the Pudding

What comes to mind when you hear the word "pudding"? Personally, I was a bit sceptical at first and suspected there might be a catch.

It turns out that the British use the term "pudding" to mean dessert, not just a specific type of dessert. It's not the shapeless, wobbly thing I had in mind!

You may find that at the end of a meal the waiter will ask, "Can I tempt you to a pudding?" which basically means, "Would you like a dessert?" It's worth noting that not all puddings are sweet and made with flour. But to keep things simple, let's list some options that fall under the "pudding" category in the UK:

— Rice pudding
— Cheesecake
— Chocolate cake or chocolate fondant
— Sponge cake with jam filling, along with a variety of sponge cakes
— Tiramisu (why not borrow it?)
— Fruit pies and crumbles
— Trifle
— And my personal favourite – sticky toffee pudding, a recipe I'm happy to share

Over time, and after hearing the waiter's question so often, the looser definition of "pudding" became a familiar term in our family and we grew to like it. The word itself is charming and endearing. Sometimes it's easier to turn down a dessert, but it's hard to resist a pudding, especially when you can taste each other's or share a portion between two.

The lingering evening is the true essence of pudding. When you've had a great time together over food and chats and find every excuse to prolong the moment before parting ways. This is frequently the case for us when we go out as a couple, and less so when our lively kids are around.

Ingredients

For 4 servings:
75 g dates
75 g softened butter
50 g brown sugar
2 eggs
1 tsp vanilla extract
140 g flour
1 tsp baking powder

For the sauce:
150 ml double cream
75 g brown sugar
25 g butter

STICKY TOFFEE PUDDING

Instructions

1. Remove the pits from the dates and chop them. In a small saucepan, bring 75 ml of water to the boil, add the dates and simmer for 3-4 minutes until they become a puree. Gently mix until smooth.

2. Preheat the oven to 180°C. Grease 4 x 150 ml pudding moulds with butter.

3. Mix the butter and sugar until fluffy, then add the eggs, vanilla, flour and baking powder. Stir in the date puree and distribute between the moulds.

4. Place the moulds into a larger dish filled halfway with boiling water, cover with tin foil and bake for 25 minutes. Check the puddings to make sure they are cooked.

5. Meanwhile, make the sauce by adding half of the cream, all of the sugar and all of the butter to a thick-based saucepan. Dissolve the sugar over a low heat, then increase the temperature and simmer. Stir until the sauce becomes smooth and thick, about 3-4 minutes. Then stir in the remaining cream.

6. Serve the puddings topped with the warm sauce and enjoy with a scoop of vanilla ice cream.

6

EDIBLE FLOWERS

Violet
\la violette\

Let's talk about another exquisite French cocktail – the violet Kir with champagne, or *Kir Impérial à la violette*. Choosing this vibrant purple drink will showcase your elegance and knowledge of the mountainous region bordering the French Riviera, known to the French as *l'arrière-pays*. I must say, I adore this picturesque part of France – with its narrow winding streets, ancient leaning stone houses and breathtaking views of the mountains, valleys and sea. It is in this region, above the bustling city of Nice, not far from Cannes and on the outskirts of the mediaeval town of Les Tourrettes, that this delicate flower with its subtle scent – the Tourrettes violet – thrives.

Make sure you visit this magical place if you get the chance. And book a table at the acclaimed Bistrot Gourmand Clovis, a gastronomic gem. And, as you enter the old part of the town, don't miss the boutique "Violettes de Tourrettes". Here, you'll find not only violet-scented perfumes, but also a variety of edible treats made from these delicate flowers.

Such treats include:

— Violet jam
— Caramel paste with violet
— Lollipops, dragées, pastilles and hard sweets made from violets
— Candied flowers and violet tea
— ...and not forgetting your cocktail-mixing ingredients – violet syrup or liqueur, which can also be used in baking or ice cream, and the potent (45°) violet Pastis which is flavoured with aniseed.

Isn't it amazing how one flower can inspire such creativity!

VIOLET CAKE

Ingredients

220 g flour
1 sachet (10 g or 1 tbsp) baking powder
60 g icing sugar
150 ml cream
30 ml milk
3 eggs
40 ml violet syrup

For the glaze:
60 g icing sugar
2 tsp violet syrup

Instructions

1. Preheat the oven to 180°C.

2. Whisk the eggs with sugar until pale. Gradually add the flour, baking powder, cream, milk and violet syrup. Mix until smooth.

3. Line a cake tin with baking paper greased with butter and pour in the mixture.

4. Bake in the middle of the oven for 30 minutes. Use a skewer to check the cake is cooked. Remove and leave to cool on a rack.

5. Prepare the glaze: in a bowl, mix the icing sugar with the violet syrup and a few drops of water. Drizzle over the cake. If desired, decorate with violet lollipop crumbs or candied violet petals.

Lavender
\crème brûlée à la lavande\

Lavender is perhaps the most romantic and visually appealing plant. I adore lavender, with its soft, enveloping violet-blue colour. Picture endless fields with a single tree or quaint building in the distance... These fragrant lavender fields are truly a symbol of Provence.

You can also find lavender in meticulously maintained English gardens, albeit a slightly different variety but equally charming nonetheless. And you'll often find another treasured flower nearby: the thistle, which is Scotland's national symbol.

Recently, I made a geographical discovery: I discovered the Royal Botanic Gardens at Kew in West London, and I must say, I was bowled over. The variety of unique flora that thrives there is simply mesmerising. In my view, Kew Gardens tops the list of London's beautifully kept gardens.

But let's not forget about the edible aspect: have you ever tasted lavender? If not, you simply must! You could sample some refreshing lavender lemonade or – my personal favourite – lavender crème brûlée.

Until I tried this dessert with its delicate and captivating lavender aroma in a town on the French Riviera, I was a loyal fan of citrus-ginger crème brûlée (a most delicious version). However, the lingering lavender essence and aftertaste truly leave a lasting impression.

And the best part is, making your own lavender crème brûlée is actually quite straightforward.

LAVENDER CRÈME BRÛLÉE

Instructions

To start, gently heat 40 ml of whipping cream with 2 teaspoons of dried lavender flowers for 15 minutes taking care not to let it boil. Next, whisk 3 egg yolks with 40 g of sugar until you have a frothy white mixture. Strain the lavender-infused cream, blend it with the yolks and mix well. Pour this mixture into small oven-proof ramekins and place them in a baking tray half-filled with water. Bake in a preheated oven at 180°C for 20 minutes. The crème brûlée is done when the centre is still slightly jiggly. Chill in the fridge for at least two hours before serving.

SUMMER PUNCH WITH ELDERFLOWER CORDIAL

Ingredients

2 bottles of white wine
300 ml ginger wine
80 ml elderflower cordial
1 litre sparkling water
4 limes, thinly sliced
3 peaches, cut into wedges
A handful of raspberries
Ice
Edible flowers to garnish (optional)

Instructions

For this amount, a 5-litre glass drinks dispenser with a tap works well. Set it up on the garden table, play your favourite tunes, lay out a range of snacks and invite your nearest and dearest to enjoy the essence of summer. Cheers!

Elderflower Cordial

A true English delight! Just picture yourself in your garden, surrounded by lovingly planted roses. Elderflower-infused drinks are the perfect thirst-quencher and wonderfully refreshing on a hot day. This syrup adds a lovely touch of floral essence to cocktails… It may sound like a sales pitch, but it really captures my inner joy.

This summer, I'm all about elderflower. I've been enjoying this high-quality, floral syrup diluted with water and served with lots of ice in a 1:10 ratio. Another simple option is to mix it with sparkling water, apple juice or a lightly sparkling apple juice.

But let's talk cocktails… You can combine it with champagne, prosecco or even gin! Sometimes, the simplest things are the best.

Here are my top three cocktails containing elderflower:

- Elderflower cordial + cucumber, mint and white wine. So refreshing!
- Elderflower cordial + white wine, sparkling water, peaches, lime, ginger and a handful of raspberries – this makes a fantastic summer punch or sangria for a light-hearted gathering.
- The "English Garden Cocktail" – a delicate mix of mint, gin, lemon juice, elderflower syrup, ice and cloudy apple juice.

PROVENCAL ADVENTURES

Truffles
\la truffe noire du Ventoux\

Every year, we eagerly anticipate the start of black truffle season. Truffles are known as *"le diamant noir"* in Provence, a name that truly reflects the value and rarity of this exquisite mushroom – a product of sheer magic. The season runs from November to early March, with the most fragrant truffles typically found from mid-December to January.

I dream of experiencing a winter's day in Carpentras, which hosts one of the largest truffle markets in France during this period. Finding this market is all about trusting your sense of smell.

Picture the scene: it's 8:30 on a Friday morning. The town at the foot of Mont Ventoux awakens under a misty sky, chilled by a frosty embrace. At the café on the square, a group wearing berets and with mysterious pouches gathers, sipping steaming espressos and engaging in lively conversation. As you approach, the air becomes filled with a potent and enduring aroma, gently teasing your senses.

At 8:45, the master of ceremonies, dressed in black from head to toe, signals the start of trading. The participants busily whisper, gesture, sniff, rub and examine the truffles. In just fifteen minutes, the traders depart with their treasure in hand.

At that moment, it's hard to fully grasp the experience. But during this brief time, the price is set, starting at 800 euros per kilogram for a decent truffle weighing 30–60 grams. Trading then moves back to the café, where the truffles are meticulously weighed and the thickness of the wad of banknotes is determined.

It would be wonderful to join a truffle hunt organised by La Truffe du Ventoux, where appetites run wild, then return to the farm for a communal dinner in front of a crackling fireplace to enjoy a menu entirely created around truffles, from the amuse bouches to the dessert.

A word of caution: fresh truffles have a short shelf life and last only a week, so enjoy them promptly or transport them swiftly. You don't want to experience a mishap like we did where our suitcase and hotel fridge were filled with the scent, only to return home to find the truffles shrivelled and dried.

TRUFFLE MASH

Ingredients

1 kg floury potatoes
80 g salted butter
70 g low-fat sour cream
½ tsp dried garlic
20 g grated Parmesan
3 tbsp milk
Truffle oil to taste
2 tbsp truffle shavings
Salt and pepper

Instructions

1. Boil the potatoes in salted water, then drain and mash.

2. Add the butter, sour cream, garlic, Parmesan and milk as required. Mix until smooth and fluffy.

3. Season with salt, pepper and truffle oil to taste.

4. Stir in the truffle shavings and serve immediately.

Cavaillon Melons
\melon de Cavaillon\

Yearning for the bright sweetness of summer sun amidst the chill, I recall a Michelin-starred restaurant in Cavaillon. This town in Haute-Provence is famed for its small melons with fragrant orange flesh, originally brought from Italy to the Papal residence in neighbouring Avignon in the 12th and 13th centuries. It seems the Popes had a soft spot for melons during their time in France.

I love Cavaillon melons, also known as Cantaloupe melons, paired with prosciutto, or simply sliced for the kids to enjoy at the beach. But one day, venturing beyond Aix-en-Provence, I discovered a restaurant called Maison Prévôt, where melons were the focus of every course – from starters, to mains and desserts.

The "tout melon" menu created by the restaurant's founder, Jean-Jacques Prévôt, has been updated over 40 times. Each year until his retirement, he found endless inspiration in this extraordinary fruit, crafting over a hundred delectable recipes. Let's explore one aromatic combination:

- Starter – fresh melon carved into a rose with smoked pike in hibiscus marinade and melon seed sauce
- Main course options – lamb tagine with melon and toasted almonds, or lobster bouillabaisse with melon
- Dessert – a treat of candied melon, almond sponge, meringue and lemon jelly with verbena

In this enchanting spot, we savoured a soft yet rich melon cocktail with aniseed called "melanis", and even took home a couple of bottles to share and enjoy on cosy, chilly evenings, enveloped in the warm aroma.

The inventive Cavaillon chef also graciously shared a simple yet enticing recipe from his repertoire.

PAN-SEARED GIANT PRAWNS WITH MELON

Ingredients

1 kg orange Cantaloupe melon
12 large giant prawns (15–20 cm in length)
Cajun spice
Butter and olive oil
1 shallot
1 tomato
1 garlic clove
Fresh lemongrass stalks

Instructions

1. Remove the shells and season the prawns with cajun spice.

2. Prepare the melon by balling or cubing it.

3. Create a quick prawn shell broth with shallot, tomato and garlic.

4. Sear the prawns in butter and oil, then set aside.

5. In the same frying pan, sauté the melon briefly, then set aside.

6. Simmer the broth for added flavour.

7. Serve 3 prawns per plate, pour the broth over and top with melon balls, then garnish with finely chopped lemongrass.

PERHAPS THE ULTIMATE DELICACY

Pan-Seared Foie Gras
\foie gras de canard poêlé\

After spending a considerable time pondering the perfect version, I find myself gazing at it with a lump in my throat – trust me, nothing compares to the unparalleled pleasure of exquisitely pan-seared, melt-in-your-mouth duck *foie gras*. You may be familiar with the common delicate pâté version which can endure in the fridge, like ours brought back from our recent trip which is patiently waiting to shine, along with some onion chutney.

As the festive season draws near, try your hand at preparing a fresh, whole liver yourself. It's simpler than you think – you just need to work up the courage.

Your dish is now ready to serve at your New Year's table. You'll be transported and immersed in the unique gastronomic culture of France. Moments like this conjure up memories of a cosy traditional restaurant, Le Coup D'Fourchette in Théoule-sur-Mer – a concealed wonder west of Cannes near the Esterel mountain range, with a small lagoon and charming beach.

The chef's culinary finesse and his wife's warm hospitality left a lasting impression on us. I have a special memory of visiting with our parents. The hosts recreated their signature dish – pan-seared *foie gras*, despite it not being on the day's menu. It was a heartwarming moment and incredibly delicious.

PAN-SEARED FOIE GRAS

Instructions

Firstly, slice the liver into 1-cm thick pieces, and season with salt and pepper. Quickly sear in butter until golden brown on both sides and pair with your favourite sweet sauce. For instance, you can create a light caramel from icing sugar, deglaze with a glass of crémant de Bourgogne, bring to the boil and let the caramel melt, then keep warm. Plate the *foie gras* on a warm dish and drizzle with the caramel. Serve with spiced bread and your preferred chutney. Besides onion, fig, blackberry or tangy pear chutney would also make a mouthwatering accompaniment.

Foie Gras Terrine
\la terrine de foie gras\

Writing about pan-seared *foie gras* wasn't in my original plan. However, after experiencing National Foie Gras Week in France, I was captivated and couldn't help myself. It was a veritable feast! The celebration brought together numerous restaurants from across the country, with chefs showcasing their skills in creating masterpieces using this extraordinary product.

Let's focus on the traditional version: *foie gras terrine*. This is what we typically envision. It's one thing to purchase a sought-after jar at a supermarket, but another to savour this culinary jewel in a restaurant.

I recall my initial encounter with *foie gras* at Ma Cuisine restaurant in Beaune – it was a wonderful surprise recommended by the owner of the hotel we were staying in. Though not the most glamorous of hotels (we were students back then), it radiated charm. The ground floor had a warm, homely feel, with a friendly dog napping under the reception desk and a cat sauntering about.

The dishes and wine served in that restaurant became a true discovery for us. The *foie gras terrine*, in particular, left a lasting impression with its subtle, elusive tenderness. The taste was creamy and buttery, the texture incredibly smooth and pleasant – a softness you wanted to linger in your mouth. Importantly, the presentation can be minimalistic, and the thickness of the slice should be generously satisfying.

Wouldn't it be intriguing to create such a terrine at home?

After much research and deliberation, I selected a recipe from renowned chef, Joël Robuchon, to guide you through. The process seems simple at first glance, but is time-consuming and requires a whole day. The key is to avoid adding any alcohol.

FOIE GRAS TERRINE

Instructions

1. Start with some fresh liver (600 g), remove the veins, cut into 2.5cm pieces and place in a deep container of very cold water with half a tablespoon of coarse salt. Cover with cling film and chill for 3 hours.

2. Then mix 8 g of salt, ¼ tsp ground pepper, ½ tsp sugar, ¼ tsp French four-spice (cinnamon, ginger, cloves and white pepper) and a pinch of ground nutmeg.

3. Remove the *foie gras* and pat dry with a paper towel. Evenly distribute the spices over the liver, place it in a ceramic baking dish, then cover again and chill for another 4 hours. Take out and shake thoroughly to spread the liver evenly.

4. Preheat the oven to 120°C and boil some water. Place the *foie gras* container into a larger dish and fill it halfway with hot water. Bake for 50 minutes.

5. Remove the terrine and drain the excess fat into a separate container, holding the *foie gras* in place with a spatula to prevent it from slipping. Carefully pour the fat back on top and leave to cool to room temperature. Cover with a lid and chill.

LEGENDARY SOUPS

Bouillabaisse
\la bouillabaisse marseillaise\

This isn't just any fish soup – it's a globally beloved delicacy that's a real showstopper at Marseille's waterfront restaurants. Picture this: a chef skilfully filleting fish, plating it elegantly, and pouring over a rich, vibrant saffron broth right before your eyes.

And guess what? There's no one-size-fits-all recipe. Every chef in Marseille claims to have their own secret technique and special ingredient. Culinary historians have traced mentions of this "fish ragout in boiling broth" back to ancient times, making it a culinary tradition that's stood the test of time.

Now, imagine booking a table for seven at the iconic Michel restaurant. You're in Marseille for business, but lunch here will be the highlight of your day – maybe even your whole trip. As you open the menu, steel yourself for jaw-dropping prices. The bouillabaisse takes centre stage, a revered dish that's tantalising and worth every penny.

The real show begins as a trolley arrives and a team of experts deftly fillets an array of fresh fish. By now, you've nibbled on aioli-dipped croutons and are ready to dive into the divine, aromatic broth that drew you here. Trust me, the experience is priceless.

Just so you can appreciate the grandeur of bouillabaisse, a portion at Michel's in Marseille will cost you 80 euros. But can you replicate the magic in your own kitchen for less? It's certainly a challenge, considering the quality of the fresh fish and the vibrant Mediterranean atmosphere that adds to the dish's allure.

I'm not attempting to recreate bouillabaisse's intricate original version here. It's a culinary masterpiece best enjoyed in the heart of Marseille, where the traditions and flavours spring to life. But why not try a simpler version that's just as captivating?

Ingredients

2 kg assorted fish (of your choice)
2 tomatoes
4 potatoes
1 leek
2 onions
4 garlic cloves
1 bouquet garni
2 fennel bulbs
300 ml dry white wine
1 pinch ground saffron
4 tbsp olive oil
Salt and pepper

EASY BOUILLABAISSE

Instructions

1. Dice the potatoes and chop the fennel and leek.

2. Sauté the onions, garlic, tomatoes, potatoes, fennel and leek in olive oil.

3. Add the fish heads, tails and backbones, white wine, water to cover, bouquet garni, salt, pepper and saffron. Cook for 30 minutes.

4. Meanwhile, marinate the fish fillets in olive oil and saffron.

5. Strain the broth, bring to the boil, add the pieces of fish and cook for another 15 minutes.

6. Serve the fish separately from the broth, with toasted baguette and garlic rouille sauce.

Onion Soup
\soupe à l'oignon\

Someone recently asked me for the ultimate onion soup recipe. Once you've tasted it, you're hooked for life, but you start noticing the finer details: sometimes it's too tangy, or needs more crispy toast and gooey cheese, or is a tad watery and missing that magical touch.

Remember that overwhelming feeling when you were first served that steaming hot bowl of soup... Where was that? Perhaps you were in a cosy traditional restaurant in Montmartre, with red-and-white chequered tablecloths, low ceilings with ancient beams, and hearty, yet pocket-friendly fare?

I can't quite recall the exact location, but I vividly remember devouring the flavourful contents of my bowl, savouring each spoonful of the onion soup – robust, emblematic, authentic and truly unforgettable. It beckons you back time and time again.

And now for the much-anticipated recipe. I sought advice from my French teacher, Mireille, known for her culinary finesse. Over our 15 years of friendship, I've marvelled at her delectable creations.

ONION SOUP

Ingredients

4 large onions
50 g butter
1 tablespoon vegetable oil
1 tablespoon flour
250 ml dry white wine
1 litre water or chicken stock
4 slices of white bread
100 g grated comté cheese
Salt and pepper

Instructions

1. Peel and slice the onions, then sauté them in butter and olive oil until golden.

2. Stir in the flour, add the white wine and boiling water, then season with salt and pepper.

3. Cover and simmer for 20 minutes over a low heat.

4. Toast the slices of bread and place them at the base of four deep oven-proof bowls. Pour in the soup, sprinkle generously with grated cheese and bake until the cheese melts.

Smoked Haddock Soup

\cullen skink\

FROM SCOTLAND

A year has passed since our Scottish adventure, where emotions ran wild and discoveries were abundant. In the middle of an unusually hot August, with London sizzling at 40°C and St Andrews in Scotland a refreshing 27°C on the beach, we did the only logical thing – donned our swimwear and braved the chilly waters of the North Sea. Sometimes, there are fantastic surprises in every climate.

One such surprise was stumbling upon the remarkable Scottish speciality, Cullen Skink, a soup made from smoked haddock. Rediscovering it again and again, each spoonful reminded me of its excellence. When I returned to seek its comforting embrace in February, I fell in love once more and couldn't help but share its tale with friends and ponder ways to make it more accessible.

It struck me that you couldn't find smoked haddock simply anywhere. Fresh from the smokehouse of a legendary coastal town, it's a mouthwatering treasure. No other fish will do – it's specifically haddock that's needed. The closest substitute might be smoked hake, but even that can be elusive.

These contemplations led to many discussions with Scottish cuisine lovers and those for whom smoked haddock was out of reach. I was still thinking about this a year later, then it dawned upon me: everyone has their own fish preferences, the only thing that matters is that the fish is hot-smoked and the results won't disappoint.

Just as it enchanted me, this soup is sure to captivate you. Even better, it is surprisingly simple to make, considering the depth of flavour it delivers.

CULLEN SKINK

Ingredients

1 tablespoon butter
1 onion (1 leek, optional)
2 medium potatoes
250 g hot-smoked haddock (or your preferred fish)
250 ml whole milk
Small bunch of chives or parsley

Instructions

1. Sauté the finely chopped onion in butter until translucent.

2. Dice and add the potatoes to the pan with 300 ml of water. Bring to the boil, reduce the heat and simmer for 15 minutes until tender.

3. In a separate pan, poach the haddock in milk for 5 minutes until tender. Flake the cooled fish, removing any bones.

4. Combine the milk, fish, onions and potatoes, and simmer gently for another 5 minutes. Season to taste.

5. Garnish with herbs before serving.

THE CROWN JEWEL

Bûche de Noël

Every year, as we immerse ourselves in the hustle and bustle of the Christmas season, we rush around buying gifts and planning festive menus. It's interesting to note that the iconic and essential menu item for the French is not a savoury dish, but a dessert – *bûche de Noël*. While the rest of the table can vary, the dessert remains a constant.

This tradition dates back to the 12th century when a beautifully cut log, often cherry wood, was specially prepared for Christmas. It was set on fire, glowing and warming the night. Over time, this symbol made its way onto the menu, but in homes with fireplaces, the tradition lives on.

There's nothing quite like the crackling embers in a fireplace. Over twenty years ago, on our first date, my husband and I discovered our recipe for happiness: a country house with a fireplace, pine trees in the garden and windows looking out over the sunset. While our dream house isn't yet a reality, every time we sit by the fire we feel one step closer to it.

But let's talk about the dessert. In France, there's fierce competition between chefs to create the most exquisite *bûche de Noël*. It's essentially a sponge roll, often chocolate but with endless variations. Some modern variations include:

Honey meringue and almond biscuit inspired by Montélimar nougat.

A giant eclair with white, red and green hard sweets featuring white chocolate and pistachio ganache with a liquid raspberry centre.

Walnut biscuit with chestnut honey, crispy walnut crust and another sponge roll flavoured with citrus and thyme.

Creamy vanilla ganache with a caramel centre, mascarpone mousse and biscuit soaked in vanilla syrup.

An exotic variation using coconut mousse with mango and passion fruit flavours.

Chestnuts and pears — a harmonious blend of fruitiness and chestnut notes.

Operation: SAVING THE BÛCHES DE NOËL

It was quite the adventure, but perhaps not the most successful… I had promised to bake two bûches de Noël for the Highgate French circle Christmas party. I found a French recipe that seemed to fit the bill. However, the world of *bûches de Noël* is vast, with each renowned French chef adding their own unique touch. I decided to stick with the classic version.

I arrived at the party with my *bûches de Noël*. They would be unveiled after the carols and I was nervous, remembering the mishaps I'd had while making them.

I had started baking the sponge layers the day before, focused on the cream after lunch, and then disaster struck! The cream melted and leaked. I couldn't fix it and my disappointment was palpable.

As evening fell and the shops were starting to close, I had no choice but to improvise. I bravely bought mascarpone, found some condensed milk, and added coffee and melted chocolate.

The carols came to an end and the moment of truth arrived. My *bûches de Noël* received glowing reviews: *"Magnifique!"*, *"Délicieux!"*, *"Excellent!"*

Credit goes to the original recipe for easy baking and rolling with a damp tea towel.

Ingredients

For the layers:
5 eggs
100 g flour
100 g sugar
1 tablespoon vanilla sugar

For the cream:
750 g mascarpone
1 can condensed milk
100 g 70% chocolate
1 teaspoon instant coffee

BÛCHE DE NOËL

Instructions

1. Whisk 4 egg yolks with the sugar and vanilla sugar until smooth. Add one whole egg and mix for a couple of minutes with a spatula. Gradually add the flour. Beat the remaining egg whites until stiff peaks form and gently fold into the mixture.

2. Line a standard rectangular baking tray with baking paper and grease it with butter. Spread the mixture onto the paper and place in a preheated oven at 200°C for 10 minutes.

3. Lightly moisten a tea towel. Remove the baked layer of sponge, place the tray on a cold surface and cover it with the towel. This makes it easier to roll it into a log.

4. Mix the mascarpone with the condensed milk. Divide the resulting cream mixture into thirds. Add the coffee to ⅔, which will be used for the inner layer. Combine the remaining ⅓ with chocolate melted with a very small amount of water.

5. Spread the light coffee cream onto the layer of sponge and roll it into a log, seam-side down. Spread the chocolate cream on top of the log to represent the log's bark. Decorate additionally as desired.

Duck for Christmas

Another Christmas in London approached, and we had already lost count of the years spent here. We took in the mesmerising light show at Kenwood House near our home. Walking the park's paths as night fell, bathed in laser beams, was truly magical. The weather had taken a turn and it was slushy underfoot with a wintery chill in the air. But instead of letting it dampen our spirits, we gathered around a roaring bonfire with the kids, indulged in pancakes and warmed our hands on steaming cups of hot chocolate. After a fun-filled evening, we returned home in high spirits but with rumbling tummies.

It was time to prepare the Christmas feast. Everyone was in a festive mood, eagerly anticipating the star of the show.

As the seasons change and the holidays race by, poultry takes centre stage on most tables. Personally, I opt for a plump farm duck for six. Goose can be a bit heavy and turkey a tad dry for my taste. But whichever bird you choose, even if it's a humble chicken, it should steal the spotlight and make mouths water as it makes its grand entrance.

While elaborate stuffings and decorations are tempting, I believe that simplicity is key, with taste being the ultimate goal. So, my go-to Christmas dish is duck with orange marmalade and I'm thrilled to share the recipe with you.

ROASTED DUCK WITH ORANGE GLAZE

Instructions

1. The night before, season the duck with salt, wrap in cling film and chill overnight.

2. Preheat the oven to 240°C. Season the duck with spices, for instance garam masala. Bake breast-side down for 15 minutes, then lower the heat to 170°C, flip the duck over and bake for another hour.

3. Mix ½ jar of orange marmalade, 2 tbsp balsamic glaze and 2 tbsp olive oil. Slice 2 oranges crosswise.

4. Remove the duck, coat it with the mixture and arrange the oranges around it.

5. Return it to the oven for another hour at 170°C.

6. Serve immediately. It's incredibly delicious!

SAY "CHEESE"

PERFECT Savoyard Fondue
\la fondue savoyarde\

Picture yourself in a magical winter wonderland in Savoie – a stunning mountain region of eastern France. After a day of strolling in the crisp, frosty air, you finally arrive back at your welcoming chalet. A fire crackles in the fireplace, casting a warm glow that reflects in your happy eyes. You're content and weary from the day's adventures, and suddenly you feel famished.

Mountain residents created the ultimate comfort dish seemingly for moments like these – cheese fondue. While historians debate its origins, many believe it hails from neighbouring Switzerland. Nevertheless, a fondue is the perfect ending to serene winter evenings.

Fondue is not only warming but brings people together. Friends and family gather around the table, using skewers to dip bread into the shared pot of cheese. White wine and heartfelt conversations accompany the meal, creating a warm atmosphere that beats away the cold outside.

What should you do with leftover cheese at the bottom of the pot? Here's a great trick: crush a shallot, crack a raw egg, pour in a shot of brandy, season with pepper and cook until it resembles scrambled eggs. Dip crusty bread into the pot to polish off the cheesy delight.

FONDUE

Instructions

Grate or cube pieces of Comté vieux (400 g), Beaufort (400 g) and Emmental de Suisse or de Savoie (200 g) cheeses. Crush a garlic clove into a special heat-resistant fondue pot called a caquelon, pour in 250 ml of dry white wine and wait for it to simmer. Gradually add the pieces of cheese, stirring until melted. Finish by mixing ground nutmeg (2 teaspoons) with 50 ml of wine and stirring it into the melted cheese.

My Find: Morbier Cheese

I have a fascinating cheese story to share with you – all about Morbier. This cheese is unique, with a rich history and a sophisticated, unconventional aroma.

For me, the most expressive cheeses in terms of scent are some Danish varieties that are a challenge to transport as they fill your suitcase with their strong smell and then assert their dominance over everything else in the fridge. Or cheeses with blue mould – not sharp in smell but in taste. Both types have a special allure and many loyal fans. Morbier, however, is intriguing because its taste is subtle and almost creamy, while its aroma is surprisingly robust, especially when aged. A true cheesy conundrum.

Morbier originates from a small village of the same name in the French mountain region of Franche-Comté. You can easily identify it by the distinctive horizontal line of wood ash running through the middle. In the past, cheese makers would take that evening's pressed milk, cover it with ash and then add a fresh batch of milk in the morning. Today, this ash layer is a nod to tradition, with the same milk used for both parts.

Opinions on such cheeses can vary widely, and sometimes even be polar opposites. Some may think the cheese is spoilt, but that's not the case! Try to embrace the unknown and savour the earthy, animalistic nuances just like we did. Your associations and emotions will surprise you. I personally felt like I was being transported to a deep, musty wine cellar or a rustic farm.

Like any other cheese, Morbier should be taken out of the fridge at least half an hour before enjoying. Make it one of the first selections from your cheese board to experience the perfect blend of strength and delicacy. Morbier also plays a prestigious role in a remarkably hearty dish called "morbiflette". This variation of the traditional "tartiflette" involves sautéing onions and bacon with boiled potatoes, then baking them with cheese until melted. Pair it with white wine from the neighbouring Jura region for a satisfying meal.

TARTIFLETTE

To make a deliciously filling traditional tartiflette for 6 people, you'll need:

Ingredients

1.5 kg potatoes
500 g smoked bacon
3 onions
2 tbsp sour cream
100 ml dry white wine
1 whole wheel of reblochon cheese
Salt and freshly ground pepper

Instructions

1. Wash and boil the potatoes in their skins until they are just tender, but not overly soft.

2. Peel and thinly slice the onions.

3. Fry the bacon in a pan until it releases its fat. Add the onions and sauté until they turn translucent. Pour in the white wine and cook until the liquid evaporates (about 5 minutes). Stir in the sour cream and cook the sauce for another 5 to 6 minutes.

4. Peel the potatoes, slice them into medium-thick rounds, and mix them with the bacon and onion mixture. Season with pepper.

5. Transfer the mixture to a large baking dish. Cut the cheese into two circles and place them on top. You can choose to remove the cheese rind if desired for a milder flavour.

6. Bake in a preheated oven at 190°C for 30 to 40 minutes. Serve hot with a side of fresh salad or green vegetables.

MANGO LIME MARMALADE

Ingredients

6 mangoes
3 limes
1 kg sugar

Instructions

1. Peel, pit and dice the mangoes.

2. Add the lime juice and zest.

3. Add the sugar and leave for 6 hours.

4. Boil and cook for 25 minutes until slightly thickened.

5. Pour into jars, seal and turn upside down.

ROQUEFORT OR SHROPSHIRE BLUE
for Breakfast?

Let's talk about blue cheeses – what a tasty topic. Remember Vanessa Paradis in that movie, enjoying Roquefort for breakfast? I adore Roquefort and dream of visiting Auvergne, its birthplace in central France. Have you been?

But, back to reality, I often head to a fabulous cheese shop near our London home in search of Roquefort substitutes. It's a small shop, but the cheeses in their compact showcase are selected with such care!

Once, I was on the hunt for English Stilton or Italian Gorgonzola Dolce. The Stilton was out of season, ripening for September. The friendly owner suggested an alternative – my new find: Shropshire Blue.

It was vibrant yellow with bold blue mould, soft and oh-so fresh – it brightened our day.

Pair it with a spicy pear chutney or experiment with other flavours. I love fig chutney with soft cheeses, or try my twist with white wine and lemon zest. Another of my favourites is mango marmalade with lime – a burst of flavour and pure joy!

A zesty accompaniment complements strong blue cheeses perfectly. Treat yourself to this flavourful experience!

Stinking Bishop: EXPECTATIONS VS REALITY

I came across this cheese with a rather unusual name while listening to my osteopath, a well-versed British lady in many respects. She wholeheartedly recommended trying this cheese. Intrigued, I delved into the history and embarked on a search. I found it surprisingly easily... and was genuinely taken aback by what I found.

You know how it goes: sometimes the experience lives up to the first impression, and other times it's sadly lacking.

Take buses for example. I'm still amazed by London's double-deckers. The whole experience of these vibrant red buses is simply exhilarating, especially from the front seats on the upper deck. The bus manoeuvres wildly on narrow streets, leaning on turns, defying the laws of physics, brushing past branches and nearly colliding with poles. The intensity of the sensations: a solid 9 out of 10.

With this cheese, the expectation was of a strong, pungent smell that should permeate from a mile away, overpowering everything else in the fridge. But it turned out not to be the case. The taste is extraordinary, elegant, not overpowering and with a hint of earthiness. Modest and more subdued than Camembert perhaps. And the aroma is unassuming. A modest 4 out of 10.

Stinking Bishop was named after a colourful character named Bishop, a farmer from the mid-19th century. He was quite the drinker with a complex personality. Legend has it he once fired a shot at a teapot on the stove because it was getting on his nerves; hence the prefix "stinking" which is more of a playful moniker meaning "unpleasant" rather than indicating smelliness.

Nevertheless, if I had to choose, I'd definitely opt for Camembert. It packs a more robust punch, with age and ripeness adding sharpness and nobility. I simply adore it, especially baked.

Ingredients

1 Camembert wheel
4-5 cloves of garlic
A few sprigs of fresh thyme
500 g new potatoes
8 bacon rashers

BAKED CAMEMBERT

Instructions

1. Boil the potatoes in their skins until tender. Drain and leave them to cool.

2. Place the Camembert in a small baking dish and score it with criss-cross markings. Fill the cheese with garlic and thyme. Bake for 20 minutes at 180°C.

3. Wrap the potato slices in bacon and fry them on a griddle pan on both sides.

4. Once the Camembert is baked, dip the bacon-wrapped potatoes into the melted cheese.

FASCINATING
FRENCH GEOGRAPHY

\Côte d'Azur en hiver

Five Reasons to Visit
THE FRENCH RIVIERA IN WINTER

We fell in love with Nice and used to visit almost every summer, but one winter we decided to see what it was like during the colder months. It turned out to be a great idea. Let me tell you why.

The abundance of light with 300 sunny days a year, intense blue sky and an azure sea that inspired great artists like Monet, Signac, Matisse, Renoir and Picasso. I'll never forget the time we grabbed a warm baguette from the bakery and enjoyed it on the beach. I wore my dark sunglasses. Despite the cool sea breeze, a scarf and a light coat, I could hardly believe it was winter. We were mesmerised by the breathtaking sunrises and sunsets, which painted a vibrant palette of colours over the sea and mountains.

The climate is mild, with temperatures ranging from 5 to 15°C during the day. It actually feels warmer outside than indoors. Our modern house in the mountains near Grasse was heated only in the main room with what seemed like a wood pellet stove. Stepping out of the shower was quite invigorating! Some brave souls, including my French friend, swim in the sea here in January (the water temperature is a bracing 13°C). But if you feel the chill and need some warmth, basking on a café terrace with your favourite aperitif is a splendid way to pass the time.

Lush greenery, palm trees and exotic plants from around the world all flourish here. I recommend visiting the picturesque micro-village of Èze, which seemingly clings to a sheer cliff, and climbing to the garden at the top for breathtaking views of the sea. The Villa Rothschild in Saint-Jean-Cap-Ferrat is also stunning and open to visitors.

During the **citrus season**, the air is filled with the vivid scents and colours of lemon and orange trees – a mid-winter joy in Menton where an annual lemon festival is held every February.

And then there's the **Mimosa season** – the ultra-yellow fluffy clusters that are nothing like winter and strongly evoke thoughts of spring. The town of Mandelieu-la-Napoule is considered the Mimosa capital and also hosts its own festival.

While reminiscing about lemon festivals, I found myself confronted with stormy British weather near a sandy beach where we spent a long weekend. The trees were bending in the gusty wind and rain was lashing against the windows. Despite the gloomy weather, I found solace in lemons, sugar, butter and egg yolks, which I used to make a mouthwatering lemon curd.

Quite simply, once you've made lemon curd yourself, you'll never be tempted by the shop-bought version again. The burst of flavour and freshness from one little jar transports you back to the sunny city and the aroma is simply intoxicating.

Ingredients

Zest of 3 lemons
100 ml fresh lemon juice
200 g sugar
6 egg yolks
120 g cold unsalted butter

LEMON CURD

Instructions

1. Separate the egg yolks from the whites and strain them through a sieve for a smooth texture.

2. Grate the lemon zest and combine it with the sugar.

3. Squeeze the lemon juice.

4. In a small saucepan, whisk the egg yolks with the sugar until the mixture lightens. Then gradually add the lemon juice.

5. Place over a low heat and continue whisking until the mixture thickens and bubbles. Be careful not to increase the heat too quickly to prevent curdling. The temperature should be enough to thicken the curd.

6. Remove from the heat, add the cold diced butter and mix well. For extra smoothness, strain the curd through a sieve.

7. Transfer to a jar with a tight lid, cover with cling film and leave to cool for 2 hours at room temperature. Store in the fridge for up to 10 days.

France Forever

I'm about to do something I've refrained from for the past couple of years – compare the incomparable: the UK and France.

We finally arrived in paradise, after years away, just for a week of the children's holidays. The morning greeted us with sunbeams softly slanting across the living room, right in the heart of Fontainebleau. Outside, through the hedge across the road, there was the same moss I once knew in the UK. But here, it feels deeper and lusher. Believe it or not, I'm a moss expert, and I can say this with confidence.

Even the freshly mown grass at the nearby castle smells different: a touch of light bitterness mingled with the mind-blowing freshness, unlike the mown grass in London's Hyde Park, which is equally inviting but drier and more tangy. The smoke from the charming stone chimneys here is sweeter and more stimulating, like a soft cloud, unlike the rare chimneys of the bustling city we're yet to return to.

Talking about food in a place where spring is warmer and the heart feels more alive is a game-changer. One bite into a baguette at a motorway service station on the way from Paris can alter your destiny: it's a different kind of sandwich, a plunge into a whirlpool of freshness and vibrancy from the ham, lettuce and eggs. And that's just a pitstop! What else lies ahead?

There's so much more to savour. A simple brasserie on a square can surprise you with an ordinary salad topped with foie gras and duck that instantly captivates and excites. So much so that your eyes light up with joy. And breakfast made with supermarket finds can last over two hours – with wonderful cheese, the freshest *jambon breton à l'ancienne* and, of course, irresistible baguettes. Can you sense the excitement?

Even lunch in the castle's cafe was prepared so exquisitely that words failed me. It's the kind of place where picking up what's left on the shelves at the end of the day is a pleasant surprise: citrus mousse, cucumber puree, delicately salted salmon and a herb-filled waffle tartlet.

It makes me yearn for a country where the sense of taste is cherished, and products and dishes are passionately discussed. A place where culinary books, maybe one on jams, lead you to plan out the year ahead just as a result of flipping through the pages.

Here's a gorgeous recipe for onion confit.

France definitely inspires, *n'est-ce pas?*

ONION CONFIT

Ingredients

1 kg yellow onions
100 g butter
200 g sugar
250 ml red wine
100 ml red wine vinegar
50 ml blackcurrant liqueur (crème de cassis)
Salt and pepper

Instructions

1. Peel and thinly slice the onions.

2. Melt the butter in a saucepan over a low heat. Add the onions and cook gently for 10 minutes. Season, add the sugar, cover and continue cooking over a very low heat for 30 minutes, stirring to avoid burning.

3. Pour in the red wine and vinegar. Cook uncovered for another 35–40 minutes until all the liquid has evaporated. Finish with a touch of crème de cassis.

4. Stir well, divide into jars and chill. Enjoy within 3 weeks.

SCOTTISH HOLIDAYS

Scotland
\une semaine en Écosse\

My little girl is napping next to me, while my son and husband are seated across the aisle. We're on a train journey home from Edinburgh to London.

The memories of this week will stay with me for months to come.

We were constantly on the go, even when we decided to take a day to unwind in the city in which we were staying. I was in a state of light-hearted excitement and my eyelashes trembled as I drifted off to sleep. Even during the day, the reality felt like a vivid dream.

Meanwhile, sheep flashed by outside and the aromatic sea breeze filled my lungs. The weather was hot, rainy and cold all at once.

- The sombre atmosphere of the city, amplified by the twilight and the echoes of yesterday's festival.
- An ancient fortress perched on a cliff, and another, restored yet steeped in history, which widened the eyes and sparked fascination.
- Seafood and fish that deserve the highest praise.
- A charming highland cow with a shaggy fringe.
- A whisky distillery – the oldest and most elegant, and noble in taste.
- Children's attractions, including a science museum which the little ones were reluctant to leave.

The list of memories seems endless. And just like the kids, I don't want to wake up and leave that colourful dream behind. I wish it wouldn't dissipate like a Scottish mountain cloud.

\haggis écossais\

Haggis, OR THROUGH SCOTLAND ON THE HANDBRAKE

Life serves up many adventures, for example, when Neapolitans send you to what they claim is the best local pizzeria. You find yourself navigating through narrow, winding streets and past hanging laundry until you come to your destination – more of an open kitchen with a couple of plastic tables than a restaurant. Surprised, you sit and they bring you pizza unlike any you've ever tasted, surpassing all others.

There was a brief introduction to my Scottish quest for the perfect haggis, their national meat dish. With only a week to work with, I ordered haggis whenever it was on the menu to give it a try, but nothing left a memorable-enough impression to continue dreaming about it.

But as fate would have it, on our penultimate day, we drove halfway to Edinburgh unsure of the smells and sounds coming from the car. We quickly veered off the motorway, realising we'd been driving along with the handbrake on.

A short way off the main road, we found a garage to fix the car and a neighbouring roadside shack, which turned out to serve the most delicious haggis in the world. Two hospitable hostesses, with enchanting Scottish accents, kindly chatted with us and rewarded us with burgers containing a juicy and tender layer of haggis.

Minced sheep offal, lungs, heart, liver, beef suet, onions and oats – not the most mouthwatering of ingredients, but trust me, the result is nothing short of amazing.

My Love,
NIGHTTIME EDINBURGH

Enchanting, damp, quirky, alive. My cherished Edinburgh. Illuminated in a soft yellow hue under the streetlamps, with traces of black from the wind and rain. This historic city boasts a youthful spirit with its theatre festivals, lively pubs, quaint souvenirs and, of course, whisky.

We stopped for just one evening to wander through the narrow, winding alleys. To soak up the lively atmosphere of a bustling pub and the chiming of the clock on the square. To breathe in the fresh sea air and let go of all our worries.

WHO SAID "CHOCOLATE"?

Chocolate Mood
\envie de chocolat\

I have a pronounced sweet tooth, and for me, chocolate – especially dark chocolate with roasted hazelnuts – is a true addiction.

Have you ever tried French chocolate croissants – *pain au chocolat?* They are a delightful starting point. I prefer them to even the most wonderful croissants with almond cream.

These pastries are simple to bake at home. Here's how: take a square of puff pastry, place two chocolate sticks parallel to the edges and roll both sides towards the middle. Then, place the pastries on a baking sheet and bake until golden brown. Enjoy them hot – it's like nothing else.

The combination of chocolate and bread is one of the most delicious. In the frugal post-war years of the 1950s and 1960s, French children had bread with butter and a slice of chocolate for a snack. The soviet version was bread and butter sprinkled with sugar.

Another excellent combination is chocolate and bananas. Slice the bananas in half, sauté lightly in butter and flambé in rum. Then, warm the bananas for 3 minutes on each side, melt the dark chocolate with a bit of water (not butter) and pour over the top. For the ultimate indulgence, top with whipped or chantilly cream.

But what I really want to share is a unique flourless chocolate cake recipe and my fail-proof brownies. And let's also talk chocolate mousse...

EVELYNE'S CHOCOLATE CAKE

Ingredients

5 eggs
100 g icing sugar
    (or 150 g to make it sweeter)
250 g dark chocolate
200 g butter
A pinch of salt

Instructions

1. Preheat the oven to 180°C.

2. Whisk the eggs with the icing sugar and salt.

3. Melt the chocolate with the butter, then combine with the egg mixture.

4. Pour the mixture into a greased baking tin and bake for 25 minutes.

Brownies!

I simply have to share that I have the perfect brownie recipe – tried, tested and incredibly delicious.

This recipe makes deliciously hearty brownies, but we've mastered the art of savouring each bite by cutting them into petite squares, which are wonderful served with a cup of aromatic espresso. Amidst the hustle and bustle – children playing or a storm brewing outside – the world comes to a standstill, focusing on that moment of bliss. It's a tranquil space filled with comfort, where everything seems to fall into place.

BROWNIES

Ingredients

150 g flour
½ tsp salt
225 g butter
170 g semi-sweet chocolate (70–80% cocoa)
180 g sugar
1 tsp vanilla extract (or vanilla sugar)
4 large eggs
120 g chopped walnuts

Instructions

1. Preheat the oven to 170°C. Grease and line a square tin.

2. Melt the butter with the chocolate over a low heat, add the sugar, then the vanilla.

3. Blend the sugar with the eggs and fold into the chocolate mix. Then fold in the flour, salt and walnuts.

4. Bake for 30 minutes – or slightly less for gooey brownies.

\la mousse au chocolat\
Chocolate Mousse
AND LIFE'S TURMOIL

Thinking back to our move to London, the whirlwind of setting up a new home and starting new schools meant putting off losing myself in tasty tales for a while.

Yet, amidst the chaos, thoughts of indulging in a light, airy delight lingered for quite some time. Imagine melting a 100-gram bar of dark chocolate in a bain marie, mixing in vanilla sugar, three egg yolks, then whisking up the remaining egg whites and folding them in gently with a silicone spatula. Transfer this magical concoction to a terrine dish to chill for at least 2 hours, and when it's ready, it feels like reaching for the stars!

But back in our London apartment, lacking a blender, suitable dish or silicone spatula, this remained a pipe dream. However, my knack for adapting to my circumstances and finding contentment in alternatives led me to a shop-bought chocolate mousse in a plastic cup. It wasn't perfect, but it did the job.

Behind the brimming cup of airy chocolate delight lies a cherished tradition: for many French families, this childhood dessert spans generations, winning hearts across the board. It's a massive hit with children, and waiters never fail to offer it upon spotting a child at the table. The whole family grabs their spoons, some hurriedly dipping into the mousse and licking their fingers, and everyone dives in together, striving to maintain some decorum.

In such moments, a yearning to be in France with the children, relishing chocolate mousse in a local restaurant, becomes almost unbearable. Their eyes light up and their cheeks flush as they savour each mouthful with pure pleasure. And if the experience falls short, a well-equipped kitchen is a must in order to whip up a homemade version.

ROASTING FANATIC

Tian: \tian provençal\ RECIPE FOR MY FAVOURITE PROVENÇAL ROASTED VEGETABLES

You might be wondering: what are the best vegetables to use when winter seems never-ending and the snow won't budge – what's on the menu? But when summer or a plentiful autumn is in full swing, vegetables come to life, bursting with flavour and aroma. While new harvests are always eagerly anticipated, for me, each season holds its own romantic charm, and with well-chosen recipes, vegetables can stay in-season all year round.

Lately, I've been captivated by roasted vegetable side dishes. At a quaint English coastal market, I was amazed by the abundance of parsnips. Roasting them alongside other root veggies was immensely satisfying. Another favourite was roasted sweet potatoes, especially when paired with guacamole. Dehydrating cherry tomatoes with garlic and rosemary was a cherished pastime. Marinating peppers in honey and balsamic added a delightful twist. And discovering a unique way to prepare courgettes – cutting them into matchsticks, roasting them, then mixing them with fresh garlic, coriander and lemon juice, seasoned with za'atar – was a definite winner. And let's not forget the aubergine, so versatile and diverse, turned into aubergine caviar or delicious baba ganoush – it's simply marvellous.

I want to share one of my favourite French side dishes that can easily shine as a main course. The colourful, light and delicious Provençal tian.

For this, you'll need 2 courgettes, 2 aubergines, 4 tomatoes and 2 red onions, preferably of a similar diameter when sliced. Although finding uniformly sized vegetables is preferable, it can be a challenge and it's not essential. It will still look authentic, and ultimately, the taste is what truly matters.

Here's the simple process: thinly slice the vegetables into rounds of equal thickness. Layer them in colourful rows in a baking dish and drizzle with olive oil. Season with salt and pepper, generously sprinkle with fresh thyme and grated garlic, then bake in an oven preheated to 180°C for an hour. You'll soon be aware of the magical aroma of thyme and garlic tantalising your taste buds.

Sunday Roast

On the list of unmissable experiences in London is visiting a gastropub for a Sunday roast.

This long-standing tradition is a heartwarming excuse to gather the family for Sunday lunch. The portions are generous and comforting, and the food warms the soul in more ways than one. It's a grand and festive affair, welcoming you to the table as part of the family.

Among the highlights is the Yorkshire pudding, which always wins out over the roasted meat and vegetables, and of course, the gravy – a sauce that completes the dish. It may seem simple, but the process behind it makes you truly appreciate the end result.

Additionally, the ambiance of traditional English pubs adds a special touch. Whether it's the one near our home, where Karl Marx is rumoured to have contemplated his works, or another by the Tower of London, which has borne witness to many historical events – dining in these establishments adds an extra layer of charm to the meal.

But if you're not eating out and are creating the meal at home, remember that besides the Yorkshire pudding, the gravy is key. I remember following Jamie Oliver's recipe with great care, vigorously rubbing some of the vegetables into the gravy, only to be met with a conservative child's refusal.

So now I keep it simple and roast a leg of lamb with garlic and rosemary, alongside vibrant and appetising root vegetables. My favourite combination includes rainbow carrots, sweet potatoes and parsnips. Glazing them with honey or adding a dash of mustard brings out their wonderful flavour.

CONCEPT:
One-Tin Roasting

In everyday life, simplicity reigns supreme, even when it comes to food. We're not always what we aspire to be, and while I may admire the culinary feats of celebrity chefs, most evenings I find myself sticking to a simple baked salmon seasoned with salt, pepper and olive oil, and accompanied by roughly chopped roasted vegetables like red onion, courgettes, peppers and tomatoes.

As I bake salmon and vegetables routinely, occasionally switching to chicken with potatoes, my family will eventually plead for something different. And at times like these, compromise is key. One-pot meals come to the rescue. Exciting, flavourful and colourful – a celebration in contrast to the mundane and ordinary. It's a feast that doesn't require extensive effort, and it's a joy to feed the family from just one dish. And the best part? Cleaning up afterwards is a breeze.

One such solution I'd love to share with you is the following recipe. Humble sausages are elevated to new heights when paired with fennel, red onions and apples, and topped with an original dressing. The result is extraordinary, delectably delicious and truly deserving of praise.

Ingredients

6–8 medium sausages
2 fennel bulbs
1 large red onion or 2 smaller ones
2 apples
50 ml dry white wine
1 tbsp liquid honey
2 tbsp olive oil
Fresh oregano leaves
Salt and pepper

ENGLISH SAUSAGES BAKED WITH FENNEL, RED ONION AND APPLES

Instructions

1. Preheat the oven to 200°C/180°C fan.

2. Peel and cut the fennel, red onion and apples into large wedges.

3. Arrange the sausages in a medium-sized roasting dish, surround them with the onion, fennel and apples. Sprinkle with fresh oregano leaves.

4. Prepare the dressing: mix the wine, honey and olive oil. Season with salt and pepper. Drizzle over the sausages and garnish.

5. Bake for 40 minutes, stirring occasionally, until the vegetables are tender and begin to caramelise. Serve with flatbreads or your favourite bread to soak up the delicious sauce.

16

OPPOSITES ATTRACT

Orange Marmalade

Remember Paddington Bear and his fondness for orange marmalade? I often feel the same way. Especially here in a city filled with shelves of citrus marmalades of every kind.

The first time I noticed this, I was taken aback and pondered over my choice. Over time and through trial and error, my favourite has become orange marmalade with ginger, with the roughly chopped rind giving it a slight bitterness. But I also adore the delicate, slightly cloudy, amber-coloured orange jam version.

Lined up ready for tasting, we had marmalade with brandy and whisky, a citrus blend and a lemon curd. These treasures and more were discovered in a quaint, authentic tea shop nearby. Chatting with the saleswoman, I learnt that the shop had just celebrated its 125th anniversary. How incredible!

And while my heart aches with nostalgia when I recall being told: *"La confiture à l'orange de Menton... est un délice"*, it truly evokes the vividness and potency of the lemons and oranges from Menton, one of the ochre-hued towns on the French Riviera close to the Italian border.

But time swiftly propels us towards new horizons. And now, Paddington Bear feels closer and clearer to me.

ORANGE MARMALADE WITH WHISKY

Ingredients

1.3 kg oranges
Juice of 2 lemons
2¼ kg white refined sugar
450 g dark muscovado sugar
150 ml whisky

Instructions

1. Place the whole oranges and lemon juice into a large pot, cover with 2 litres of water and bring to the boil. Simmer for 2 hours until the orange peel is tender.

2. Drain the water into another pot and set to one side. Scoop out the orange pulp, including the seeds and pith, and combine with the water. Bring to the boil and cook for 6 minutes, then strain through a sieve.

3. Finely chop the orange peel, combine with the white and muscovado sugar and the orange pulp liquid. Cook over a low heat until the sugar dissolves, then boil vigorously for 15–25 minutes. Add the whisky, remove the foam and store in jars.

MY IMPRESSIONS OF LONDON *and Marmite*

When I first arrived in London, I never anticipated that:

- Juice will always be served with ice
- Burgers could be so delicious
- After a year, litter in the street would feel familiar
- Freedom of expression in terms of clothing is disarming, relaxing and makes you want to fit in
- Multiculturalism isn't hidden but boldly emphasised and celebrated
- Under certain circumstances, you wouldn't need your own car for two years
- Arriving with three suitcases and a cat, then gradually acquiring everything, including a full set of furniture with a single click, is entirely feasible
- I'd become an expert in moving and be able to provide advice
- Even after such a long time, there would still be mysteries, like Marmite!

I thought to myself that, after two years, I had adapted to the British healthcare system, yet I had never tried Marmite. Perhaps out of fear of pulling a face and not understanding its appeal. Those who have tried it are fiercely divided into ardent fans and staunch haters. It's even marketed with the slogan "Love it or hate it".

To delve deeper, one day my husband and I were returning from a school event, descending sharply down a narrow street from a lush hill. It was very damp and fresh, although the rain had already stopped, and we walked carefreely, chatting and laughing in the evening emptiness.

"Wait, let's enjoy this beauty and freshness", he said, ever the romantic. I paused and took a breath, but realised that the dampness now seemed mundane.

Most likely, compared to the moist climate of Holland, where we studied at a young age, and the almost heavenly weather in France, we have stopped being impressed because – I'm almost afraid to say it, but it's true – in London, we feel at home. Whereas before, our stay always felt temporary.

But let's get back to Marmite. Thinking of where home now is pushed me to finally try this wonderful spread with its numerous health benefits. It's essentially yeast extract, rich in B vitamins and folic acid. Some British people don't go a day without having Marmite on toast for breakfast.

The key is not to have it straight from the jar, but to first spread hot bread with salted butter, then apply a thin layer of Marmite on top. This way, you won't be shocked by its, let's face it, unique taste.

Tart and thick, thick and tart. It will definitely excite your taste buds and wake you up at the start of any gloomy day.

SEAFOOD SENSATIONS

Langoustines
FROM THE BAY OUTSIDE

I had to write something on this, but words were catastrophically lacking. We'd been living in this seaside location for almost two years, yet our experiences with seafood were sadly insufficient.
Until we were presented with this generous portion of langoustines for lunch.

Plump, yet robust and springy. Tender, yet full of character. Meaty and painstakingly extracted from their shells. They are best generously drizzled with lemon juice for that extra zest, and are even more heartening with a glass of Chenin Blanc.

The view from the window overlooking the harbour in this small fishing town is stunning. Boats sway on the greenish-blue water and rare cars make their way along the cliff.

The sea darkened, reflecting the sky, and it became cooler. Something happened inside me, and that plate of langoustines made my heart pound.

I am not exaggerating. In that precise moment it was apparent that happiness lies in food.

New Year's Lobster

The tree stood tired and sparkling, having fulfilled its festive duty. Some of our neighbours had already taken their trees down.

On New Year's Eve, I went to the fish market, stood in a long queue and overheard the other customers ordering lobster. I thought: this is a sign.

I had been eyeing them up for a while, passing the aquariums in the fishmongers on my way to music classes with my little one. On any other day, only a couple of lobsters would be languishing in their compartment. But now, for the Christmas period, there was a whole pool of them.

And there was me, willing and able to transform anything into a gourmet dish, set the right mood and impress my main admirer – my husband.

It would have been better if the lobster I got had been caught locally. They say the Dorset Blue lobster is especially good. Mine was from Canada, and I hoped it wouldn't be inferior to its British cousin.

As it turned out, I was right to choose a smaller lobster – they taste better than the larger ones as their meat is firmer.

But how do you cook it? Boil it for 12 minutes in salted water. I won't share more to avoid the graphic details. Suffice it to say that my fingers were trembling with nerves.

You can serve lobster hot or cold. Keep seasoning to a minimum so as not to overshadow the delicate flavour of the meat. A spritz of lemon works well with cold lobster, while hot lobster pairs nicely with garlic butter and a hint of parsley.

We've endured some challenging times and look hopefully towards the future. We deserve to indulge ourselves!

Aioli
\aïoli\

The greatest joy of a seaside holiday, in my opinion, is freshly caught fish – being spoilt every evening with an abundance of fish starters and main courses, including tuna, prawns, scallops, octopus, sea bass, turbot and sea bream, which have been plucked straight from the sea onto your plate, quickly passing through the kitchen and still winking at you mischievously.

It's not just dinner, but a lingering pleasure, someone please stop me! It's impossible to handle such luxury without some emotional overheating!

Accompany your choice of fish with the colourful sauce "aioli", which is essentially garlic mayonnaise. This sauce sets the mood and tone of your meal. In the south of France, it's served in the centre of a huge dish, surrounded by vegetables and fish, and the name "aioli" there refers not only to the sauce but to the dish as a whole.

This dish is central to my memories of Marseille and Upper Provence – that sparkling association, a definite moment of truth when events fall into place. While aioli may seem universal and widely used in Mediterranean cuisine, I lovingly cherish memories of its Marseille version.

Let's prepare this simple and delicious sauce, surround it with baked fish and a vegetable garnish. A classic combination is potatoes, carrots, green beans, artichokes and cauliflower, but you can also create your own unique interpretation. Simply cook and revel in the creation of a light and healthy dish.

AIOLI

Ingredients

2 garlic cloves
350 ml olive oil
1 egg yolk
½ lemon
Salt and pepper

Instructions

1. Prepare a large wooden or stone mortar and pestle. Crush the garlic and grind it until it forms a smooth paste. Add a pinch of salt, the egg yolk and a splash of lemon juice.

2. Gradually add olive oil, while vigorously stirring the mixture with the pestle in one direction. The result should be a sauce resembling mayonnaise but slightly thicker in consistency.

3. If you can't blend the sauce using this traditional method, don't worry, you can always use a blender – although true aioli purists might not agree!

FIVE O'CLOCK TEA

Afternoon Tea at F&M

After six months of dreaming, planning and hoping, I finally experienced afternoon tea at one of London's most iconic locations – Fortnum & Mason's flagship store in Piccadilly.

From reservations falling through to missed opportunities, it felt like fate had finally smiled upon us. By some stroke of luck, my friend and I found ourselves on a tour and needed somewhere to have lunch. It all aligned perfectly: a sought-after table, a classic afternoon tea stand with finger sandwiches, fluffy scones with jam and clotted cream, and a choice of sweet desserts or savoury canapes, all accompanied by a unique selection of teas and a glass of champagne.

On the bottom tier of the stand were delicate finger sandwiches – thin strips of soft bread with fillings such as ham and cheese, cucumber with a creamy chive spread and coronation chicken. Each tiny sandwich was surprisingly satisfying.

The next level held scones. I was feeling quite full, but scones are perhaps the most enchanting English pastry, usually served with jam and clotted cream or occasionally with onion chutney and cream cheese for a savoury twist. I have a soft spot for scones, and so searched for a recipe to try at home.

On the top tier was an array of sweet desserts or savoury treats, depending on your chosen menu. It's impossible to devour everything, but you're here for a celebration and a touch of ceremony, so you sample a bit of everything and savour the moment.

It's worth noting that the F&M store boasts over 300 years of history and offers the most spectacular food hampers, which make a classy gift.

The store and the afternoon tea are a bit on the pricey side, but the experience is truly magical – from the clinking saucers to the genuine smiles of the waiting staff, and not forgetting the beauty and taste of the food!

I highly recommend a visit.

CLASSIC ENGLISH SCONES

Ingredients

500 g flour, plus some for dusting
1½ tbsp baking powder
½ tsp salt
125 g unsalted butter
100 g caster sugar
180 g whole milk
75 g raisins (optional)
1 egg yolk for brushing
Jam and clotted cream for serving

Instructions

1. Sift the flour and baking powder into a large bowl. Add the salt and cubed butter. Rub the mixture between your fingers until it resembles bread crumbs. Add the sugar and combine. Make a well in the centre and pour in the milk, then, if desired, add raisins. Quickly mix with a table knife until you reach a smooth consistency.

2. Preheat the oven to 200°C/180°C fan. Dust the work surface with flour and place the dough onto it. Lightly dust a rolling pin with flour and roll the dough out to a thickness of about 3 cm. Dust the edge of a 6cm-diameter glass with flour and cut out 16 circles. Line a baking tray with baking paper and place the dough circles onto it. Brush each one with beaten egg yolk.

3. Bake in the oven for 12 minutes until the scones have risen and turned golden brown on all sides. Once ready, transfer them to a wire rack and leave them to cool for 5 minutes, then slice in half and serve with jam and clotted cream.

Earl Grey:
THE STORY OF OUR RELATIONSHIP

Do you remember the first time you tried Earl Grey tea with its distinctive bergamot flavour? For me, it was a revelation. This memorable event took place at a Pioneer Camp in the early 1990s, when my parents sent me a letter with a few Twinings Earl Grey tea bags tucked into the envelope.

The aroma was so unique, soft and captivating that I don't even recall the contents of the letter. It was probably about love. But the lasting impression for me was the taste of bergamot.

My affinity grew stronger as I explored different variations, not just with milk but also with a hint of mint, added to the intense Tetley tea bags for example. Fast forward to France in our first year, where guests seated at a long table praised my tea highly.

After a few disappointing experiences with various brands, I eventually found a wonderful tea from Teapigs here in the UK. Their Earl Grey range offers both strong and light versions, delicate with blue flowers, just as the "medium premium" segment should be.

I recently had the pleasure of visiting the legendary Mariage Frères tea shop. Despite being French, it's often noted as one of the best places in London to purchase tea as a gift.

While making my purchase, I was surrounded by chaos – two hungry children demanding burgers! It was hard to focus on the wall of mysterious jars behind the counter. I didn't want to make a mistake. In the end, I impulsively chose Earl Grey Imperiale and Earl Grey French Blue, and my joy knew no bounds.

Deep breath, slow exhale, and relax... Aromatherapy and a sprinkle of optimism in a delightful cup. The simple things are the best.

THE PERFECT DINNER

Onion Confit
\confit d'oignons\

This is something that truly inspires me. The whole onion theme is just incredible: I adore French onion soup, and a dish called *pissaladière*, and have a special fondness for a French *confit* or *confiture d'oignon*, or onion chutney or marmalade as it's called in the UK.

I feel like life wouldn't be complete without discovering the marvellous harmony that onion chutney brings to meat dishes. A small dollop is traditionally served with *foie gras* and it is also sublime paired with beef liver.

The plethora of nuanced flavours here are crucial, both sweet and tangy, not to mention the texture and colour – finding the perfect jar can be a quest in itself. So, when I stumbled upon a recipe in my favourite French culinary magazine for liver with onion and date confit, I knew it was a match made in culinary heaven.

We had just returned from our first year in France, brimming with excitement and new experiences. I decided to invite my dad, who is no longer with us, for lunch. Despite not being a fan of liver, my dad praised my culinary creation so much that it remains a cherished moment, as his ultimate approval of my culinary skills. It's a heartwarming memory tied to a successful recipe.

It is true that the British also appreciate the magic of caramelised onions. Who would have thought that burgers with caramelised onions and blue cheese could be so delicious?

Ingredients

4 pieces of beef liver, about 150 g each
3 onions
120 g pitted dates
20 g sugar
150 ml apple cider vinegar
60 g butter
1 pack of green salad
Olive oil
Balsamic vinegar or cream
Salt and pepper

LIVER WITH ONION AND DATE CONFIT

Instructions

1. Peel and thinly slice the onions. Sauté them for about 10 minutes until soft and golden in 20 g of butter.

2. Dice the dates and add them to the onions. Season with salt, pepper and sugar. Let them caramelise for 20 minutes over a very low heat, stirring occasionally.

3. Season the liver pieces with salt and pepper and fry them for 2 minutes on each side in a mixture of olive oil and 20 g of butter. Transfer to a plate.

4. Pour the vinegar into the pan that the liver was cooked in. Reduce by half. Add the remaining 20 g of butter in small pieces and stir.

5. Return the liver pieces to the pan and heat for 2 minutes.

6. Serve with the onion and date confit and green salad (*frisée* works best), lightly drizzled with olive oil and balsamic vinegar.

I can already imagine the shower of compliments coming your way!

Irish Stew

It's been about 15 years since this recipe became a staple in my repertoire of go-to dishes. Considering the number of times I've served it since then, with everyone always asking for seconds, my Irish stew deserves a medal for its resilience and popularity.

The secret is simple: it's all about the extra flavours: onions, garlic and rosemary. This trio, well-known in many British recipes, combined with high-quality lamb fillet and the bold flavour of carrots, creates a harmonious balance. And of course, a sprinkle of salt and pepper – but that's a given.

Let's jump right into it without further introduction.

IRISH STEW

Ingredients

800 g lamb fillet
700 g carrots
1.5 kg potatoes
2 onions
1 whole garlic
3 sprigs of rosemary
1 generous bunch of coriander (50 g)
Salt and pepper

Instructions

1. Cut the lamb into medium-sized pieces.

2. Chop the onion, and peel and crush the garlic. Use either pre-peeled baby carrots or peel and cut standard carrots into chunks.

3. Sauté the onion and garlic. Add the meat and rosemary leaves, and season with salt and pepper. Brown the meat well on all sides in a large pot.

4. Add the carrots, stir and cook for another 7 minutes.

5. Peel and roughly chop the potatoes, then add them to the pot. Cover with water and season with salt. Simmer over a medium heat, partially covered with a lid, for about 30 minutes. Occasionally check how the liquid is being absorbed, ensuring the stew doesn't burn.

6. At the end of cooking, add the finely chopped coriander, then stir, remove from the heat and serve.

20

FRENCH CLUB CHALLENGES

Galettes des Rois
\galettes des rois à la frangipane\

This marks my second culinary escapade during my time with the French club, a local interest group formed of residents from our area. After receiving praise for my *bûches de Noël*, I was promptly tasked with baking galettes. Once again, I felt a flutter of nerves, wondering if I could rise to the occasion.

Perhaps I need to work on my flair for drama, but the tasks entrusted by this club and their approval somehow strike a chord with me. Especially as there's an abundance of recipes for this traditional French post-Christmas treat. After meticulously studying them all, I opted to follow a tried-and-tested recipe from a fellow club member, simply adding a drop of rum to the filling.

But let me tell you what these galettes are all about. They have a rich history which dates back to Ancient Rome. It's mind-boggling!

These treats are prepared for a celebration on 6 January symbolising the arrival of the Three Kings in Bethlehem. A large dried bean was traditionally tucked inside, which nowadays is typically a porcelain or plastic bean or small figurine. The person who discovers it in their slice is crowned king or queen for the day.

In families with children, the youngest crawls under the table and decides who gets the next slice. As you can imagine, children absolutely adore this tradition.

What's fascinating is that even at Louis XIV's table the king was chosen with a galette. A galette is made each year for the President of the Republic, however it doesn't contain a bean as this would contradict the principles of equality and fraternity. During the French Revolution, for obvious reasons, the galette was no longer referred to as royal, and instead became known as *Galette de l'Egalité*, or Equality Cake.

The most delightful part of the King's Cake is the filling, which is made of ground almonds, named frangipane in honour of an Italian count with the same name who gifted this recipe to Catherine de Medici. A splendid gesture, I must say.

My galettes at the event were devoured to the last crumb, and every guest who indulged in them came over to express their gratitude.

GALETTES DES ROIS

Ingredients

For the filling:
500 g ground almonds
400 g sugar
100 g softened butter
3 large or 4 medium eggs
Zest and juice of 1 lemon
A drop of rum (to taste)

Instructions

1. Combine all the ingredients. Prepare two rolls of puff pastry. Cut out circles slightly larger than the radius of the baking tin. Lay one circle in the base of the tin and prick it with a fork.

2. Carefully spoon in the filling, cover with the second circle and pinch the edges to close. Create a design on the top with a knife and make a small hole in the centre to act as a "chimney".

3. Glaze with apricot jam. Bake at 180°C for 35 minutes. Leave to cool before serving.

Mini Quiches
FOR THE FRENCH CLUB

The melodious preludes of Debussy resonate in my ears, complemented by the kind words of members of the local French community who relished my mini quiches. It feels like a grand piano concert, with just a dozen of us today. Yet there are thirty quiches: a true feast.

I baked them with care after being tasked with preparing savoury canapes, and chose to make them as I thought "what could be more French?" Quiches are the most wonderful tartlets which can have various fillings, enveloped in an egg and cream mixture and sprinkled with grated cheese before a brief 15-minute stint in the oven.

We once visited Mireille, my French "mum", as I lovingly call her, in a village bordering the Fontainebleau forest. We were ravenously hungry and she greeted us with a delightful, still-warm courgette quiche. She placed it on the table and inadvertently left my husband alone with it.

We engaged in lively kitchen banter for about a quarter of an hour, then returned to the living room, where the fireplace crackled, only to discover that my husband had demolished all but one slice. It was quite awkward! The entire sizable dish had vanished almost in an instant.

Since then, I've learnt the delicious art of French home cooking. And so I attempted to replicate the same effect for a slightly larger group, using a muffin tin with 12 wells. To make 30 small quiches, I had to bake three batches.

THREE TYPES OF MINI QUICHES FOR A LARGE GATHERING

Instructions

1. For the first batch, I finely chopped and sautéed one onion, 200 g of bacon and 250 g of mushrooms. For the second batch, I thinly sliced and sautéed 500 g of courgettes, adding two grated cloves of garlic and half a bunch of coriander at the end. For the third half-batch, I kept it simple and mashed a 200-g can of canned salmon with a fork and added chives.

2. Next, I combined 300 g of sour cream, 300 g of double cream and six lightly beaten eggs. I seasoned both the mixture and fillings with salt and pepper, then cut out circles of the desired size from ready-made sheets of puff pastry and lined the moulds with them.

3. I pricked the bottoms with a fork and started by spooning in the filling, followed by pouring the egg mixture and sprinkling with grated cheese: different batches with either cheddar or mozzarella.

4. I then baked them for 5 minutes at 210°C, then another 10 minutes at 170°C.

ENGLAND CALLING

Strawberry Fields
OF THE BEATLES

"Let me take you down
'Cause I'm going to strawberry fields
Nothing is real
And nothing to get hung about
Strawberry fields forever"

The melody is playing in my headphones, performed by a classical orchestra. The Beatles' songs conjure up all sorts of memories and associations and Strawberry Fields has a special magic and mysterious charm for me. I really loved a book called "Les Beatles, comment les cuisiner" by French culinary critic and Beatles fan Emmanuel Rubin. He asked some famous French chefs and amateur cooks to come up with recipes inspired by 12 hits from the legendary pop group.

It turned out to be quite interesting:

- The song Penny Lane is represented by a recipe for fish and chips. But not just any fish and chips – it includes a batter made from white beer, flour, cornflour and sparkling water.
- Octopus' Garden is rendered as a dish of octopus with a garlic and saffron sauce called *rouille*.
- Glass Onion inspires a recipe for onions stewed with elderflower.

And as for Strawberry Fields... This classic masterpiece deserves nothing less than an unforgettable recipe for strawberry cupcakes. Soft and incredibly delicious.

Ingredients

For about 18 cupcakes:

For the batter:
360 g flour
2 tsp baking powder
¼ tsp baking soda
½ tsp salt
230 g butter at room temperature
300 g sugar
3 eggs
1 tbsp vanilla extract
120 g sour cream
120 ml full-fat milk
220 g strawberries

For the icing:
340 g butter
¼ tsp salt
700 g icing sugar
100 g strawberries, plus extra for decoration
½ tsp vanilla extract

STRAWBERRY CUPCAKES

Instructions

1. Mix the flour with the baking powder, baking soda and salt.

2. Take the butter out of the fridge and let it soften. Cut it into small pieces and beat with the sugar until light and creamy.

3. Add the eggs one by one, mixing well. Add the vanilla extract.

4. Gradually add the flour in thirds. Mix well again.

5. In a separate bowl, mix the sour cream with the milk, then fold it into the batter.

6. Chop the strawberries finely and fold them into the smooth batter.

7. Line a muffin tin with cupcake liners and fill them with the batter. Bake in a preheated oven at 180°C for 20-25 minutes. Leave them to cool.

8. For the icing, beat the butter with the salt and icing sugar.

9. Add the strawberry puree and vanilla extract. Mix well. Pipe the icing onto the cupcakes and decorate with strawberry slices.

BRITISH CULINARY NAMES OF *French Origin*

Who would have thought that some of the most quintessentially British food names like bacon, toast, custard and stew actually have French origins? Let's take a little linguistic adventure together:

Bacon. Bacon is a must-have ingredient in British breakfasts and many other dishes. But its original name, pronounced with a French accent, dates back to the 14th-century French language. Back then, it simply meant cured pork meat.

Toast. The British adore toasted bread, and almost anything can go on toast, especially beans! So, as much as we'd like to believe in its noble British roots, we have to face the truth: the French verb "toaster" means to bake or toast on a grill.

Custard. Even the sweet sauce so commonly used in the UK, known as custard or *crème anglaise* in France, has its roots in the French word "coutarde", which eventually evolved into "crustarde" meaning "covered with a crust".

Stew. A favourite British way to cook is stewing. Whether it's meat with vegetables or just veggies, it results in a warm and comforting dish called stew. However, the word comes from the Old French word "estuver", meaning "to immerse in hot water".

But the history of borrowing culinary names doesn't stop there. Rumour has it that some British dishes actually hail from France. There are even whispers about the famous Yorkshire pudding.

Renowned English chef Fanny Cradock once mentioned on a TV show in the 1970s that British cuisine is so unoriginal that even the Yorkshire pudding (that traditionally accompanies a Sunday roast) has Burgundian origins.

This caused quite a commotion. Yet it's entirely possible that recipes from neighbouring countries, with such intertwined histories, have borrowed from each other.

No matter how surprising or doubtful this geographical tale may seem, the beauty and significance of Yorkshire puddings remain unchanged. So, why not try making them yourself?

YORKSHIRE PUDDINGS

Ingredients

140 g flour
4 eggs
200 ml milk
Sunflower oil
Salt and pepper

Instructions

1. Preheat the oven to 230°C/210°C fan.

2. Pour some sunflower oil into each well in your muffin tin, then place the tins in the oven to heat up.

3. Sift the flour into a bowl and add the eggs. Mix until smooth.

4. Gradually pour in the milk, stirring vigorously until smooth. Season with salt and pepper.

5. Transfer the batter into a jug, then carefully remove the hot tins from the oven. Pour the batter into the cups.

6. Return the tins to the oven and bake for 20–25 minutes until the puddings have risen and turned golden brown. Remember: don't open the oven while baking!

7. Serve straight away.

Picnic on the Beach:
ALWAYS WITH FISH AND CHIPS

We had another wonderful day by the sea with the family, taking deep breaths of the fresh sea air and feeling the sea salt on our skin. It was a lovely day in May, on the English coast just over the channel from France.

At times, we sought shelter from the cool breeze behind a row of houses in a quaint little town. But we kept returning to the pebble beach to play with the kids. We built sandcastles, buried ourselves in the pebbles, sorted stones by colour and tossed them into the foamy waves.

Although one of the closest beaches to London is at Brighton, this time we visited Deal in Kent, where we once spent a wonderful couple of winter months. From there, we could see the striking white cliffs that jut out into the sea, almost transporting us to another time zone: our phones automatically adjusted an hour ahead and roaming notifications popped up.

Historically, Deal was a port known for smugglers, adding a touch of romance. Even today, hidden treasures are said to be found in the walls of the charming, crooked houses.

A must-do tradition for us at the seaside is indulging in a generous portion of fish and chips, freshly fried in bubbling oil just over the road from the pier. This dish is so filling that greedy seagulls eagerly circle above, hoping for a share of the leftovers.

Unfortunately, fish and chips just isn't the same for me without the sea, the wind, the seagulls and the sky. Despite its iconic status, this dish won't necessarily make you fall in love with England. The fish is often quite plain and not overly seasoned. But the sea breeze adds its own special flavour. Ultimately, whether it's perfectly seasoned or not, it doesn't matter much to us or the seagulls.

On a brighter note, I made a unique discovery of vegan fish and chips in Brighton, made from seaweed and tofu – they were surprisingly delicious!

TOP FIVE
London Restaurants

I'll be honest, our favourite pastime, no matter where we are, is exploring restaurants. I remember a French acquaintance, while keeping tabs on our whereabouts, once exclaimed "Mais, vous êtes toujours au restaurant!" And she was right (about 95% of the time). Our most memorable moments always involved us seated at a table with cutlery in hand. It's like a break from being at home, a chance to unwind and discover new flavours, often driven by curiosity about others' culinary creations. And a particular pleasure is savouring expertly prepared food – it really adds a touch of joy to life.

In London, we've been fortunate to find some great dining spots. You can truly relax here, and dine out or order in constantly until you feel like trying your hand at cooking. And if inspiration hits rock bottom, you can always venture out in search of it once again.

But the huge variety out there comes with exceptions. For instance, we're not fans of chain restaurants. We feel they lack the chef's personal touch. And the shortlist of our favourite places, which I'd like to share with you, doesn't include the myriad national restaurants spread across the UK. Though they certainly include some interesting finds...

So, from our modest perspective as seasoned lovers of France, appreciating originality and style, here are our top five favourite restaurants in London:

Flagship Ottolenghi Restaurant: ROVI. We waited two weeks until we miraculously snagged a table. But the experience was well worth the wait. For those unfamiliar with Yotam Ottolenghi, he's a vibrant London chef of Middle Eastern descent who completely revolutionised my view of gastronomy. The explosion of colours and vegetable and spice combinations he creates is truly unique.

Best steak on Charlotte Street: We often find ourselves on this street, a culinary haven. Amidst a variety of eateries, Sicilian Bricco e Bacco stands out. The tantalising aroma of juicy steaks wafting out can be sensed from afar. Tempting, hearty and perfectly cooked steaks – a hedonist's dream straight out of a "Matrix" movie. When asked about allergies, we jokingly replied we had none, except for being vegetarians. The waiter chuckled, albeit not immediately.

Exquisite dining on the 37th floor in the City: One of my birthdays was meticulously planned by my grown-up daughter. It was a day filled with her creative surprises and love, featuring a magical garden corner in the park, an immersive art exhibition, a gastro-bus and, for lunch, a high-end restaurant in the iconic Sky Garden atop a London City skyscraper. The Fenchurch restaurant left an indelible impression with its dish preparation and presentation.

Excellent French bistro in Marylebone: Blandford Comptoir boasts modern design and authentic French cuisine, making it ideal for business lunches and romantic dinners. The charming area around it, with a street lined with French brands and authentic restaurants, is a feast for the eyes and a delight for the palate.

Appetising grilled chicken in Notting Hill: Cocotte Rotisserie. We adore this spot for its inventive take on simple chicken. However, seating is limited and reservations are a challenge, and delivery orders fly out swiftly. Apart from the flavourful chicken, their truffle mash and quality sides and snacks are definitely worth a try.

As I write this, it was perhaps our best culinary experience to date.

Untouristy England
IN THE COTSWOLDS

I often envision English villages shrouded in misty clouds, adorned with whimsical, slightly askew stone cottages that transport me to the enchanting ambiance of... rural France. Near Oxford lies a unique place: the Cotswolds, a collection of small yet vibrant villages, with renowned eateries, bustling main streets and a charming cheese shop showcasing a delightful array of local cheeses and also a sprinkling of French cheeses.

It's worth noting that London boasts beautifully manicured botanical gardens and parks. Take Kew Gardens, for instance – it's not just a park, it's a marvel that holds a special place in my heart. With its allure and relatively low tourist traffic, this park could easily be dubbed a hidden gem on my list. Especially in spring, when the whole place bursts into bloom.

Oxford and Cambridge, with their striking architecture and lively student scenes, are undeniably alluring. Oxford even boasts a fabulous botanical garden of its own.

But the villages in Cotswolds – they're my one true love.

You see, living in a bustling city brimming with life, sometimes all I crave is a break from the urban buzz and crowds, and even from the convenience: the shops, takeaways, restaurants and cafes. I yearn for wide-open spaces, fresh oxygen, untamed gardens and farms. A place where mobile signals falter, internet lags and the rustling of book pages by a crackling fireplace fills the air. And where half the ingredients for dinner are plucked fresh from your very own garden.

On one of those serene evenings, I'd happily whip up a garden risotto with this next straightforward recipe.

GARDEN RISOTTO

Ingredients

300 g Arborio rice
1 large onion
2 glasses dry white wine
About 1 litre of chicken stock
6 cloves of garlic
About 300 g each of green and yellow courgettes
Zest of 1 lemon
About 200 g each of frozen green peas and green beans
100 g grated Parmesan cheese
5 sprigs of mint
Olive oil and butter
Salt and pepper to taste

Instructions

1. Prepare the chicken stock (by simmering ½ chicken or its carcass).

2. Sauté the finely chopped onion in a mix of olive oil and butter. Add a glass of wine, the rice and a couple of ladles of fresh stock. Cook until the rice is done, stirring and adding stock as needed. Season with salt if required.

3. In a separate pan, sauté the garlic and add the sliced courgettes. Pour in another glass of wine, the lemon zest, salt and pepper. Let it simmer, then combine it with the rice.

4. Sauté the green peas and beans separately, then add to the pot.

5. Mix well, stir in the Parmesan, garnish with mint and serve immediately.

Burgers: Yes, Please!

My children absolutely adore British burgers, and truth be told, we have become quite the fans ourselves. But let's dive into this somewhat controversial topic from a different perspective.

Now, for some reason, I never really noticed wisteria – that lush purple ivy – in London before. When I lived in the Swiss Cottage area, it was all about magnolias, cherries and lilacs. But after moving to Highgate, it was like a veil had been lifted from my eyes: I noticed those pale, dreamy clusters adorning every facade. I found myself both delighted and puzzled – it felt just like being in France! Back there, this ivy had grown beautifully over the gates of our house, becoming a romantic symbol for me.

I also recall the first time I took my daughter for an entrance exam at the school we moved north for. After the taxi drove off, leaving me behind a wall of rain, I searched for a cafe to pass the time. Arriving at a crossroads, I couldn't spot anything promising. I retreated under a sprawling tree and spent a wet, miserable hour there.

But then, how unexpectedly vibrant that neighbourhood turned out to be! It was like an emotional love song! Cafes, shops, smiles from passersby, our home which I filled with furniture and accessories – it had been completely empty before we arrived. Misty mornings, the golden hour, starlit nights. A life constantly buzzing with energy.

Now, what does this journey into the unknown have to do with burgers? Let's address this head-on. In the past, I might have wrinkled my nose and firmly declared: no to burgers. Give me high-end French cuisine instead. Yet, after adjusting to life in the UK, I realised that the burgers here are incredibly tasty. Not your average fast-food fare, but rather gourmet burgers crafted as art.

Picture this: a burger featuring a flawlessly grilled meat patty topped with onion chutney and blue cheese. Or my personal favourite – a burger with a giant prawn, avocado and sweet chilli sauce. These are burgers that you can customise to your liking. Gluten-free buns, salad instead of bun – all readily available almost everywhere and delivered in about 20 minutes. Naturally, the kids often stage a strike, insisting on their own burgers. And sometimes, it's hard for me to resist.

One of the juiciest and most unique burgers I've discovered on London's cosmopolitan streets is the Hawaiian burger with teriyaki sauce and grilled pineapple.

Fun fact: In the Victorian era in England, the pineapple symbolised wealth and prosperity, and it still adorns St Paul's Cathedral. Such was its rarity that people didn't eat it, but rented it out for celebrations.

GRILLED PINEAPPLE BURGER

Ingredients

For homemade teriyaki sauce:
200 ml water
50 ml soy sauce
50 g brown sugar
2 tbsp honey
2 tbsp sesame seeds
1 tsp fresh grated ginger
½ tsp garlic powder
2 tbsp cornflour

For 4 burgers:
450 g minced beef
½ tsp sesame oil
½ tsp salt and pepper
½ tsp smoked paprika
4 round burger buns
8 slices of fresh pineapple
4 slices of cheddar cheese
8 lettuce leaves
Optional: 1 red onion, salt, juice of ½ lemon and 1 tomato

Instructions

1. Start by preparing the teriyaki sauce. Mix the water, soy sauce, sugar, honey, toasted sesame seeds, grated ginger and garlic powder. Heat gently, then add cornflour to thicken. Adjust the consistency as needed. Remove from the heat and leave to cool for 15 minutes.

2. Toast the burger buns in a toaster or on a grill. Grill the pineapple until grill marks appear.

3. Mix the sesame oil into the mince, then shape it into 4 patties. Season with salt, pepper and paprika. Grill for 4 minutes on each side over a medium-high heat. Top with a slice of cheddar and allow it to melt slightly.

4. Assemble the burgers: slice the buns, place lettuce leaves on the bottom bun, add the meat patty with cheese and pineapple slice. Drizzle with teriyaki sauce. Optionally, add a slice of tomato and red onion: thinly slice and marinate briefly in lemon juice and salt. Top with the other half of the bun and serve warm.

STRANGEST British Dishes

In British cuisine, the term "pie" isn't always what you might expect, and "pudding" doesn't always mean what you think. Sounds a bit odd, right? Let's unravel this culinary mystery with some intriguing dishes that deserve a closer look, each with a unique name.

Pigs in blankets
Can you guess what this dish is all about? Here's a clue: it's like a quirky twist on a Russian salad called "Herring under a fur coat". But in this case, it's mini sausages snugly wrapped in bacon blankets and pan-fried to perfection. Simple yet delicious, whether served as a snack or a tempting side dish.

Toad in the hole
Imagine those same sausages, nestled and baked within a giant Yorkshire pudding. This is a savoury delight made from a batter of flour, eggs and milk, seasoned with salt and pepper. Who would have thought that this combo would work so well? And despite its amusing name, there's no toad involved in this culinary creation.

Jellied eels
Here's a surprisingly tasty treat – eel served in a flavourful jelly. It's best enjoyed in the fresh sea breeze, sitting by a seafood stall, perched on a wobbly plastic chair, watching passersby stroll along the seafront.

Mushy peas
A classic British side dish consisting of mashed green peas. Often paired with the iconic fish and chips, mushy peas add a flavourful touch to complete the meal. Simply soak dried peas overnight, then boil and mash them with a touch of salt, pepper, butter, fresh mint and a splash of lemon juice. A delightful and traditional invention.

Black pudding
Just as Yorkshire pudding isn't a dessert, black pudding isn't a sweet treat either. It's actually a type of blood sausage. The name might be puzzling, but this dish is

quite popular and even rather fashionable. Served in restaurants alongside asparagus, roasted rhubarb, celery, scallops, or paired with potatoes and tangy tomato chutney.

British Pub Culture
AND SHEPHERD'S PIE

You know what a major contrast is between the UK and America? In America, there are just a few pubs, while in the UK, they are scattered across the map like a painted canvas.

In Highgate, our small neighbourhood in North London, there are a whopping 35 pubs. It's a tiny area, and we're still puzzled by how so many cosy spots exist here. Pubs range from simple watering holes to more gastronomic delights, each with its own unique menu and ambiance.

Once, we ventured to explore an old building on the main route into Highgate. With just one lane left due to the road narrowing, cars lined up in both directions. We were genuinely curious about the perpetual traffic jam. As it turns out, there's an ancient pub there with incredibly delicious food, like artichoke soup that made us forget all about the road.

When one of Highgate's pubs could no longer keep up financially and closed its doors, the locals were deeply saddened. "How can you close a pub?" they lamented. "It's not just a place to eat; it's where souls come to relax and connect!"

Another interesting titbit is that after a certain time, usually after 8, pubs often don't allow children. This rule can apply during the day too; if you have a teenage daughter, she can't sit in the bar. A 12-year-old girl may be asked if she's 18 and then politely directed to a corner near the entrance or to another room. Those rules can be set in stone in certain establishments.

My overall take on pubs is this: comfy leather seats, slightly sticky tables, a crackling fireplace and quirky wall art. It's lively, loud and full of charm. After a while, you start to really enjoy the atmosphere. For a hearty lunch at a gastro-pub, I usually go for one of the pies. My top pick is Shepherd's pie. It's not your typical pie but a savoury delight of minced meat topped with creamy mashed potatoes. Simple, delicious and oh-so satisfying.

SHEPHERD'S PIE

Ingredients

1 onion
2–3 medium carrots
500 g lamb mince
2 tbsp tomato paste
A splash of Worcestershire sauce
500 ml beef stock
900 g potatoes
Milk and butter
Vegetable oil
Salt and pepper

Instructions

1. Chop the onion and carrots, then sauté in vegetable oil. Add the lamb mince, season, brown and drain any excess fat.

2. Stir in the tomato paste and Worcestershire sauce, then simmer for 7 minutes. Pour in the stock, bring to the boil, then leave it to simmer for 40 minutes.

3. Meanwhile, make the mashed potatoes and preheat the oven to 180°C.

4. Spoon the mince into a baking dish, top with the mashed potatoes and create ridges with a fork. Bake for 20 minutes until the potato edges brown.

Recipe Index

\France\

ENTRÉE
Marinated Artichokes 29
Hot Oysters 40
Foie Gras Terrine 91
Mini Quiches 207
Easy Bouillabaisse 96-97
Onion Soup 100
Onion Confit 139

PLAT PRINCIPAL
Potato Gratin 17
Leek Gratin 20
Tian 161-162
Pan-Seared Foie Gras 89
Duck in a Reduced Orange Sauce 38
Roasted Duck with Orange Glaze 114
Liver with Onion and Date Confit 196-197
Provencal-Style Sea Bream with Tapenade 44
Pan-Seared Giant Prawns with Melon 85
Aioli 183
Fondue 119
Tartiflette 122
Baked Camembert 128-129

DESSERT
Bûche de Noël 110-111
Spiced Honey Cake 62
Violet Cake 71
Galettes des Rois 205
Frozen Nougat 59
Lavender Crème Brûlée 73
Chocolate Cake 150
Chocolate Mousse 156

\UK\

STARTERS
Quinoa, Mango and Sugar Snap Pea Salad 32-33
Mango and Prawn Salad with Sweet Chilli Sauce 51
Scottish Smoked Haddock Soup 103

MAINS
Truffle Mash 81
Garden Risotto 225
Irish Stew 199
Sausages Baked with Fennel, Red Onion and Apples 166-167
Shepherd's Pie 233
Grilled Pineapple Burger 228
Gravy 23
Yorkshire Puddings 217

AFTERS
Brownies 154-155
Strawberry Cupcakes 212-213
Sticky Toffee Pudding 64-65
Classic English Scones 189
Lemon Curd 134-135
Mango Lime Marmalade 124
Orange Marmalade with Whisky 172
Custard 22
Summer Punch with Elderflower Cordial 74

KRISTINABABI.COM